A Feast for the Eyes

Recipes from America's Grandest Victorian Neighborhood

by David Dominé

Photography by Robert Pieroni

Acknowledgements

This book is a work of neighborhood pride, something that couldn't have come about without the hard work, dedication and support of many people. I'd like to thank neighborhood organizations such as the Fourth Street Neighborhood Association and especially the firm of Franklin, Gray & White, PSC for its generous assistance in making this project a reality.

In addition, I'd like to extend my gratitude to the members of the committee who worked so hard to get this cookbook on the shelves. Thank you to Herb Warren, Gayle Warren, and Gary Kleier, for spearheading this effort, and thank you to Marry Morrow and Earlene Zimlich for their administrative skills. I'd also like to express my appreciation to Juliet Bianca for her invaluable help collecting the recipes and to Kim Crum, who was a faithful editorial sidekick while writing this book. Thank you as well to Jim Redmon for his assistance and input in the planning stages of this book.

And of course, there are all the homeowners who graciously opened their doors – and their recipe books – to provide a glimpse of the hospitality that awaits you in Old Louisville, America's grandest Victorian neighborhood. Thank you and bon appétit!

Copyright © 2010 by David Dominé
Photograph Copyright © 2010 by Robert Pieroni

13-digit International Standard Book Number	978-1-934898-09-3
Library of Congress Card Catalog Number	2010926481

Cover design and book layout by James Asher Graphics
Photography by Robert Pieroni

Manufactured in the United States of America

All book order correspondence should be addressed to:

McClanahan Publishing House, Inc.
P.O. Box 100
Kuttawa, KY 42055

800-544-6959

www.kybooks.com

McCLANAHAN
PUBLISHING HOUSE
INCORPORATED

Book Committee

David Dominé	author, editor, food stylist
Herb Warren	co-chair
Gayle Waren	co-chair
Gary Kleier	co-chair
Kimberly Crum	contributing author, recipe editor, proof reader
Juliet Bianca	recipe editor
Mary Morrow	treasurer
Earlene Zimlich	administrator

Introduction

Old Louisville is a treasure waiting to be discovered. Wherever you stroll – even after you've been here for years – it seems that there's always something new that will catch your eye: a hidden gable, a bit of ornamental carving, a stained-glass window you hadn't noticed before. Take a tour of this grand American neighborhood, and you'll come to realize that Old Louisville is indeed a feast for the eyes – both outside and inside the hundreds of grand mansions, townhomes and apartment houses that pepper its tree-lined streets and alleys.

In addition to wrought-iron fences, elaborate façades and ornate front doors, you'll find impressive grand stairwells, hand-carved fireplaces, intricate hardwood floors and other myriad details that make Old Louisville rooms some of the most splendid in the nation. Inviting parlors, entry halls, bedrooms, foyers, bathrooms and libraries all embody a level of craftsmanship and attention to detail not seen in most modern homes today, however it is in the kitchens, breakfast nooks and dining areas where the true sense of hospitality lives on. Whether it's an elegant 1880s town house, a sprawling mansion from the 1890s, or charming turn-of-the-century condo, Old Louisville lives around the dinner table.

The places where meals are cooked and enjoyed form the heart of the house and this is where family recipes are passed on, traditions are started and stories are shared. It's where holidays are observed and in Old Louisville it's also where yearly events such as the Kentucky Derby, the Holiday House Tour and the St. James Court Art Show are celebrated.

This sense of hospitality and a pride of ownership live on today in *A Feast for the Eyes: Recipes from America's Grandest Victorian Neighborhood.* Thanks to more than 30 generous homeowners and famed entertainers in the neighborhood, an enticing glimpse of life inside some of Old Louisville's most beautiful homes has been preserved in these pages. Not only will you find great original recipes and beautiful color photography of the dishes prepared, you'll see stunning interiors and snippets of the architectural details that make Old Louisville one of the most handsome neighborhoods in the country. In addition, you'll learn about residents from the past and present who have made the neighborhood what it is today. So sit back, fix yourself a plate and enjoy a taste of America's grandest Victorian neighborhood.

Table of Contents

The Southern Exposition

Before there was an Old Louisville, before there were the hundreds of grand residences that define the neighborhood today, there was the Southern Extension. A largely undeveloped tract of land immediately to the south of Louisville proper, the Southern Extension was chosen by the Louisville Board of Trade in the early 1880s as the location of an impressive wooden structure with mechanical, scientific and cultural displays touting the South's most famous product, cotton. The Southern Exposition, as it was known, opened its doors in 1883 and, for five consecutive seasons, from August to October, it welcomed visitors from around the world. During the first 88 days alone, three quarters of a million people made the trip to the famed Southern Exposition in Kentucky's largest city. Not even a hundred years old, Louisville had about 120,000 inhabitants at the time.

A highlight of this early world's fair proved to be the incandescent light bulb, a recent invention of former Louisville resident Thomas Edison. Said to be the world's largest public display of electric lighting at the time – there were 4,600 lamps in the exhibit hall alone – the Southern Exposition was a major catalyst in the growth of interior electric lighting around the globe. By the time the exposition closed in late 1887, Louisville had grown by leaps and bounds, many of its finest homes already outfitted with electrical wiring.

As it turns out, the outskirts of the burgeoning city had expanded well into the Southern Extension by the time the massive exhibit hall was dismantled, and the footprint left by the 600 x 900-square-foot building proved to be the ideal base for a ritzy new suburb. The Victoria Land Grant Company was formed and parcels of prime real estate were sold off to the movers and shakers of Louisville. Triggering a building boom that would last for the next 20 years, they employed the finest architects and craftsmen in the region – and the area soon emerged as an elegant suburban neighborhood replete with parks, walking courts, shady boulevards, gas lamps, and, of course, wonderful homes.

THE ALICE HEGAN RICE HOUSE

One of the many reasons Maria Eckerle loves her Neoclassical home on St. James Court is the history. "You can sit here in the evening and imagine the poetry that was read, the music that was played and the famous people who visited, such as Ernest Hemingway." Like most of the homes in Old Louisville, the Alice Hegan Rice House has a story to tell; but in this case, it has many stories to tell. In the three decades bestselling author Alice Hegan Rice took up residence there, she penned numerous books that garnered her fame at home and abroad. In addition, her husband Cale Young Rice was a noted poet and playwright who authored some of his most influential works during this time.

Once described as "a bit of country in the heart of town," the mansion still preserves a sense of calm today, another reason why Maria loves to call it home. According to Alice Hegan Rice in her autobiography *The Inky Way*, the rambling house was built around 1910 and "adapted to our particular needs. Two large workrooms and a maximum of quiet were first to be thought of."

Maria, in turn, has adapted the residence to her needs, the most notable of which includes lots of room for her big game trophies. A stuffed zebra head – she shot it in Zimbabwe – presides on a pedestal in the hallway, one of the many visual reminders of the home's most recent occupant. Maria, a former opera major, looks forward to many more years in Old Louisville and plans on having lots of stories of her own to tell.

Bibb Lettuce with Roast Duck and Black-Eyed Peas

Among the many organizations that Maria Eckerle supports is Kentucky Hunters for the Hungry, a non-profit, volunteer-run organization comprised of responsible hunters and conservationists who encourage the donation of venison for homeless shelters and food banks throughout the state. Given her passion for hunting, it's not surprising that wild game is often on the menu when she entertains at home. This elegant salad pairs tender Bibb lettuce and black-eyed peas – two Kentucky favorites – with meaty slices of roast duck breast infused with a tangy marinade. For a sophisticated country supper, enjoy with a glass of hearty red wine such as zinfandel or syrah.

2 large boneless duck breasts
2 cups cream sherry
2 cups reduced-salt soy sauce
1/2 cup lime juice
1/2 cup diced jalapeño pepper
1/2 cup chopped white onion
1/2 cup diced celery
1/2 cup diced carrot
3 tablespoons olive oil, divided
Kosher salt and cracked black pepper
1 large head Bibb lettuce
2 cups cooked black-eyed peas
1 tablespoon apple cider vinegar

Score the skin on the duck and place in bowl with the sherry, soy sauce, lime juice, jalapeño, onion, celery and carrot; cover and marinate for at least 4 hours. Heat 2 tablespoons of olive oil in a Dutch oven over medium heat and season the duck with salt and pepper. Pan sear 4 minutes on each side, cover and place the Dutch oven in an oven preheated to 450 degrees; cook for 15 minutes or until the middle of the duck reaches 150 degrees. (Depending on how rare you like the duck, you may want to cook it longer.) Cool the breasts and thinly slice. Assemble individual salads by topping several leaves of Bibb lettuce with slices of duck and several spoonfuls of black-eyed peas dressed with the 1 tablespoon olive oil and the apple cider vinegar and seasoned with salt and pepper. Garnish with diced carrot, if desired, and enjoy. Serves 6.

Chicken Croquettes

In *Mrs. Wiggs of the Cabbage Patch*, the most famous of the Alice Hegan Rice books, Uncle Bob, a well-to-do friend, invites the family out to dinner at a nearby restaurant. One of the dishes they enjoy is chicken croquettes, a popular Victorian treat that has largely fallen out of fashion in this country. Try this straight forward recipe, and it will become part of your regular culinary repertoire.

2 tablespoons salted butter
1/4 cup finely diced celery
1/4 cup finely chopped white onion
2 heaping tablespoons all-purpose flour
1 cup whole milk
1/4 teaspoon dried thyme
1/8 teaspoon freshly grated nutmeg
1/4 teaspoon kosher salt
2 large boneless chicken breasts, poached
1/2 cup all-purpose flour
2 small eggs, beaten
1 1/2 cups fresh bread crumbs
3 cups canola oil for frying

Melt the butter in a saucepan over medium-low heat and sauté the celery and onion until soft; stir in the 2 tablespoons flour and cook the mixture for 2 minutes. Turn up the heat to medium and slowly whisk in the milk, stirring constantly until the mixture thickens. Stir in the thyme, nutmeg, and salt and let cool. Finely chop the chicken breasts (there should be around 3½ cups) and stir into the cream sauce. Transfer into a bowl and let chill, uncovered, for at least 4 hours in the refrigerator. To assemble to croquettes, divide the chicken mixture into 12 equal portions and shape each into a cylindrical form. Coat each cylinder with flour and dip in the beaten egg before rolling in crumbs to coat. Lay the croquettes out on a cookie sheet and chill in the refrigerator for 3 hours. Fry in hot oil immediately prior to serving and drain on paper towels; enjoy warm. Serves 6.

THE AMELIA FIELDEN HOUSE

One of the best-kept secrets in Old Louisville is the secluded square of land bounded by Sixth and Seven streets to the east and west, and Park and Ormsby avenues to the north and south. Locals know it as Floral Terrace, and it's one of several charming walking courts found in the historic district today. Walking courts – they're also called pedestrian courts – are a remnant of Old Louisville's Victorian heyday, when developers included narrow park-like strips of land instead of streets in some areas to create inviting green spaces for residents and outsiders alike. Developed in 1905, Floral Terrace is one of the newest walking courts in the neighborhood.

Dwellings on Floral Terrace, such as the charming home of Gary and Diane Kleier, came about as variations on a single plan called a four square, with variety achieved by rotating the floor plans, changing porch styles, and using different roof styles. The first occupant of the Kleier's home, a widow by the name of Amelia Fielden, bought the property in 1910 and resided in the house till 1934, when it was bequeathed to her daughter.

Like most residents in Old Louisville, Diane and Gary take custodianship of a historic property very seriously; however, they realize that homes sometimes need to change with the times. Gary, an expert in historic preservation, recently oversaw extensive renovations that maintained the structure's architectural integrity while adapting it for use in a green century. The end result is an inviting retreat perfect for evenings alone or for leisurely dinners with friends.

Gary's Spicy Corn Chowder

This hearty soup has a zesty bite from modest amounts of jalapeño and cayenne pepper, but the Kleier's guests never find it too spicy. Gary recommends tasting the chowder before the addition of the cayenne pepper at the end and adjusting accordingly. Gary and Diane often add dried pepper flakes for an extra punch.

5 slices bacon, cut into 1/4-inch strips
1 medium yellow onion, finely chopped
1 medium red bell pepper,
   seeded and finely chopped
1 medium jalapeño pepper,
   seeded and finely chopped
4 cloves garlic, minced
1/4 cup all-purpose flour
4 cups chicken stock
3 large unpeeled red potatoes, diced
1 teaspoon kosher salt
1/2 teaspoon freshly ground black pepper
1 cup heavy cream
3 cups frozen corn kernels
1/4 teaspoon cayenne pepper
1 bay leaf

In a soup pot over medium heat, fry the bacon until crisp. Remove with a slotted spoon and drain on a paper towel; reserve for garnish. Add the onions and red pepper to the pot and sauté until tender, about 4 minutes. Add the jalapeño pepper and garlic and sauté for 1 minute. Whisk in the flour, stirring continuously until thoroughly combined and very light brown. Add the chicken stock, potatoes, salt and pepper and stir to combine. Simmer for 10 minutes and add the cream, corn kernels, cayenne pepper and bay leaf. Cook for 20 minutes more. Correct the seasoning before ladling into deep bowls and garnishing with the bacon. Serves 6.

Roasted Garlic and Rosemary Potatoes

Diane has always been a fan of potatoes in all shapes and sizes. About 15 years ago she created this recipe by combining several of her favorite recipes into this one, which is sure to become one of your favorites.

3 pounds unpeeled small
   red potatoes, diced
Juice and zest of 1 lemon
1 teaspoon kosher salt
1 teaspoon freshly ground
   black pepper
4 large cloves garlic, minced
1/4 cup coarsely chopped
   fresh rosemary
1/3 cup extra light olive oil
1/4 cup grated Parmesan cheese

Preheat oven to 425 degrees. In a large bowl, toss the potatoes with the lemon juice, lemon zest, salt, pepper, garlic and rosemary. When thoroughly coated, drizzle in the olive oil and toss again. Coat a shallow casserole with a spray of vegetable oil and distribute potatoes evenly over the bottom; bake for 45 minutes or until golden brown, turning once or twice. Remove from the oven and sprinkle with the grated Parmesan cheese. Place under the broiler until the Parmesan melts and turns golden brown. Before serving, sprinkle with additional salt and pepper to taste, and garnish with rosemary sprigs. Serves 6.

AUGUSTUS E. WILLSON HOUSE

Clarke and Loomis, Louisville's premier architectural firm of the late Victorian era, designed this Italianate mansion just south of Central Park in the 1890s. Its first resident, Augustus Willson, was governor of Kentucky from 1907 to 1911 and he is remembered for declaring martial law in western Kentucky tobacco-farming counties during the Black Patch Tobacco Wars. Although the beleaguered Republican politician reportedly died in the home, owners Jim and Linda Brooks, are happy to report no hauntings today.

The Brooks are especially proud of the mansion's many elegant details, which include original wooden night shutters and classical motifs such as the egg and dart, the green man, scrolls, scallops and fleur-de-lis in the abundant terra cotta ornamentation on the façade. Another highlight is the intricate wood inlay on the central staircase and newel post, which features a laurel motif carried over from the exterior to the stained glass window on the landing. The preservation of these details is a result of careful stewardship by its owners; only five families have owned this lovely Fourth Street home in its more than 115 years of existence.

Architectural Note: A newel is the upright central post that the steps of a circular staircase wind around. In stairs having straight flights, it is the principal post at the foot of the staircase or the intermediate posts in the center.

Zesty Apple Sauce

According to Linda, this recipe inspired by the Barefoot Contessa is labor-intensive but worth the effort. The combination of citrus zest and two types of apples creates a complex flavor lacking in everyday apple sauce.

Juice and zest of 2 large navel oranges
Juice and zest of 1 large lemon
3 pounds Granny Smith apples
3 pounds Winesap apples
1/2 cup firmly packed dark brown sugar
4 tablespoons salted butter
2 teaspoons ground cinnamon
1/2 teaspoon ground allspice

Preheat oven to 400 degrees and place the zest and juice of the oranges and lemon in a large bowl. Peel, quarter, and core the apples and toss them in the juice, reserving the peel of 2 of the red apples. Add the peel and transfer to a non-reactive Dutch oven or enameled iron pot; stir in the brown sugar, butter, cinnamon and allspice and cover. Bake for 1 hour, or until all the apples are soft, and stir with a whisk to make a chunky sauce. Serve warm or at room temperature. Serves 8.

15

Rice Mélange

The recipe for this savory side, retrieved from an old *Southern Living Magazine*, is a Brooks family holiday favorite. They enjoy it with beef tenderloin.

1 1/4 cups beef consommé
1 1/4 cups canned French onion
   soup, undiluted
1/2 cup melted butter
1 1/2 cups uncooked long grain
   white rice
1/2 pound button mushrooms,
   sliced

In large bowl, combine all ingredients and stir well; pour into a lightly greased, 2-quart baking dish. Cover and bake for 1 hour and 10 minutes in an oven preheated to 325 degrees. Serves 8.

AUSTIN'S INN PLACE

Just a few blocks from downtown Louisville, this lovely pair of buildings from the 1880s is a testament to the value of historic preservation – and the dedication of an enterprising young man who rescued the roof-challenged houses in the 1990s. Today's owners, Tom and Mary Austin, used walkways to unify the Italianate townhouses and transformed them into a comfortable bed and breakfast inn that welcomes visitors from around the world. Among the many amenities is a full-service bar – despite the fact that early resident Augustus Willson, Kentucky's 36th governor, won his office running on a Temperance platform. Apart from a cozy breakfast alcove, guests of the Austins can enjoy a morning repast or afternoon snack in one of two elegant dining rooms where Mary likes to display her sense of southern hospitality.

To reserve your room, contact Tom and Mary Austin at:
Austin's Inn Place Bed and Breakfast
915 South First Street
Louisville, Kentucky 40203
(502) 585-8855
http://www.austinsinnplace.com

A Taste for Politics

Governor Augustus Willson is not the only historical figure associated with Austin's Inn Place. Willson was a junior partner in the Louisville firm of John Marshall Harlan, before Harlan became a U.S. Supreme Court justice in 1877. Lewis Dembitz, lawyer and beloved uncle of Louis Dembitz Brandeis, lived there as well. Brandeis would serve as Supreme Court Justice from 1916 to 1939.

18

Asparagus Vichyssoise

4 cups chicken broth
3/4 pound fresh asparagus,
   trimmed and chopped
6 medium red potatoes,
   scrubbed and diced with peels
1 leek, cut into small pieces
1 small yellow onion, chopped
3/4 teaspoon kosher salt
1/2 teaspoon ground pepper
8 ounces cream cheese
Fresh chives or scallions for garnish

An improvisation on a classic, Mary Austin's version can be enjoyed hot or cold.

In a soup pot, bring the chicken broth, asparagus, potatoes, leek, onion, salt and pepper to a boil and simmer for 15 minutes, or until the potatoes are fork tender. Add the cream cheese, cut into cubes, and use an immersion blender to purée to the desired consistency. Correct the seasoning and warm through for 5 minutes on the stove. Ladle into bowls and sprinkle with chopped chives or green onion. Serves 6.

Neptune Salad

On its own or as a filling for sandwiches, Mary often serves this seafood salad to her lunch guests. For an economical alternative to lump crab, use imitation crabmeat.

2 cups real mayonnaise
3 teaspoons prepared horseradish
1/2 cup chopped yellow onion
1 cup finely diced celery
1/2 teaspoon salt
3/4 teaspoon ground white pepper
2 pounds crab meat
2 cups frozen peas, thawed

In a large bowl, mix together the mayonnaise, horseradish, onion, celery, salt and white pepper and gently stir in the crab and peas. Refrigerate for at least an hour and serve on a bed of romaine lettuce garnished with olives and vegetable crudité. Serves 6 to 8.

Spinach Parmesan Clusters

A dear friend, the late Roz Leiner of Atlanta, shared this tasty appetizer with the Austins. Prepared in advance, the clusters can be frozen and served later.

3 cups frozen chopped
   spinach, thawed
2 cups herb seasoned
   stuffing mix
2 small yellow onions,
   finely chopped
6 large eggs, beaten
1/2 cup finely chopped
   water chestnuts
3/4 cup butter, melted
1 cup grated
   Parmesan cheese
1 tablespoon garlic salt
1 tablespoon Accent
1/2 teaspoon dried thyme
1/2 teaspoon black pepper
10 dashes Tabasco sauce

Cook spinach according to package directions, cool and strain. Squeeze out excess moisture and combine in a mixing bowl with the remaining ingredients. Shape into balls about 1 inch in diameter and place on a baking sheet lined with parchment paper. Bake at 350 degrees for 20 minutes. Makes about 50 clusters.

BECKURT HOUSE

The Richardsonian Romanesque architectural style was modern in the late 1880s, when this home was built for Herman Beckurt, the president of Anderson and Nelson Distilleries. The façade features heavy stonework, arched windows and a recessed entrance. Though once divided into apartments, the residence has retained its original Victorian charm and details such as elaborate roseate woodwork and original stained glass windows can be found throughout the interior of the mansion today. With five bedrooms and eight fireplaces, the Beckurt House is a comfortable dwelling for owners Joseph and Juliet Bianca and their four dogs. Heirloom furniture from the French Quarter New Orleans home of Joseph Bianca's great grandparents enhances the aesthetic appeal of this grand Victorian mansion.

Deviled Eggs with Red Caviar

This recipe challenges the stereotype of deviled eggs as a dish for summer picnics and potluck suppers. The addition of red caviar and a garnish of green chives transform a pale traditional side dish to a vivid and elegant holiday appetizer or anytime treat.

12 large hard-cooked eggs
3 medium shallots, minced
2 tablespoons butter
1/2 cup sour cream
1/3 cup mayonnaise
1 1/4 teaspoons kosher salt
1/8 teaspoon cayenne pepper
1/4 cup finely chopped
   fresh chives
Zest of 3 lemons, finely grated
3 tablespoons red caviar, chilled

Peel the eggs under running water and cut lengthwise into halves. Remove the yolks and set aside in a mixing bowl. Slice a small piece from the bottom center of each egg so it won't move after the plate is filled. In a small skillet, sauté the shallots in butter over medium-high heat until soft, about 2 minutes. Mash the yolks with a fork and mix in the sour cream, mayonnaise, salt, and cayenne pepper. Add shallots and combine. Pipe or spoon the filling into each indentation and generously sprinkle each stuffed egg with chives and lemon zest. Immediately prior to serving, garnish each deviled egg with a spoon of caviar. Makes 24.

Orchestral Tiramisu

Now a Bianca family favorite, this dessert recipe originated with the Junior Group of the Dallas Symphony Orchestra in 1983. A tempting blend of espresso, brandy, chocolate and sweet mascarpone, this treat was a favorite at gourmet dinners for patrons of the symphony. "Trust a gathering of classical music enthusiasts to know their tiramisu," says Juliet.

2 tablespoons instant espresso
1 cup hot water
8 tablespoons brandy, divided in half
2 cups whipping cream
1 cup sugar
16 ounces mascarpone cheese
2 large eggs yolks
2 dozen lady fingers
2 tablespoons cocoa powder

Set a medium-size bowl (or the bowl of electric mixer) in the freezer to chill. In a pie pan, dissolve espresso powder in hot water. Stir in half of the brandy and set aside. In the chilled bowl, whip cream with an electric mixer on high until peaks form. Add sugar, mascarpone cheese, egg yolks, and remaining brandy, and beat at medium speed until combined. Then, beat on high speed until thick and fluffy.

To assemble the dessert, take a third of the lady fingers and dip each into the espresso mixture, coating both sides without letting them get soggy. Place the ladyfingers side-by-side in the bottom of a large glass bowl. Spread a third of the mascarpone mixture on top and sift a third of the cocoa powder on top of that. Repeat this process two more times. Chill until ready to serve, at least 2 hours. Spoon into martini glasses for an attractive presentation. Serves 12.

BELGRAVIA COURT

Just a stone's throw from Joseph and Juliet Bianca's beautiful Fourth Street home sits one of Old Louisville's most charming walking courts. An innovative concept that ensured an extra sliver of green space in a bustling city neighborhood, Belgravia Court became the Louisville's first pedestrians-only, or walking, court in 1892. Illuminated by gaslight 24 hours a day, a grassy boulevard with double sidewalks transverses the north end of St. James Court from Fourth to Sixth streets, affording its residents an idyllic park-like setting at their own front doors. The elaborate and stately residence of Sean and Kevin Williams greets strollers who enter Belgravia Court from the east gate. Constructed in 1897, the French Châteauesque masterpiece was once home to famed distiller William Wathen.

25

THE BENJAMIN STRAUSS HOUSE

Built in 1896 for prominent dry goods magnate Benjamin Strauss, this three-story Italianate mansion on Third Avenue, the "millionaires row" of Victorian Louisville, has been restored to the grandeur a millionaire would have expected. Inside, the foyer communicates an elegant first impression, with visitors immediately taking note of ornate inlaid wood floors and a huge oaken mantel with carved koi pillars. The impressive balustrade leads to glittering rectangular stained-glass windows with wreath-and-ribbon motifs typical of the era. Kim and David Mowder, the current owners, have topped the original newel posts with antique bronze lamps of the nymphs, Autumn and Winter.

The impressive foyer makes it difficult to imagine what the Mowders saw on their first visit to the house. In addition to broken windows and a large hole in the floor, formerly grand doorways had been covered over with dry wall. Fortunately, the house had good bones, and within four years of their purchase, the Mowders had rehabilitated and restored the 5,800-square-foot mansion. Much of their labor involved refinishing elaborate in-laid parquet floors and reconditioning birds-eye maple, cherry and oak finishes throughout, and they scoured antique malls in several states for period pieces and replacement porcelain tiles for nine working fireplaces. Their efforts have paid off handsomely and the result is a home that is not just an elegant retreat, but a warm and inviting place to entertain friends and family.

Company Corn

David Mowder created this simple dish for the grill and adapted the recipe for the oven when it was too cold for grilling. He and Kim now use the oven all the time, since the oven cooks more evenly than the grill. The recipe does not use salt and is a favorite of their health-conscious friends.

6 ears white corn on the cob
1/3 cup olive oil
5 cloves garlic
1 teaspoon fresh chopped basil

Preheat the oven to 400 degrees. Clean the corn, removing husks and silks. Combine the olive oil, garlic, and basil in a small bowl, and place each ear of corn on a piece of aluminum foil that measures roughly 10 inches by 5 inches. Use a basting brush to evenly coat each ear of corn with the olive oil mixture; wrap each ear, ensuring that the foil is twisted tightly on the ends and is long enough to stretch across the width of an 8-by-11-inch baking pan. Drape the wrapped ears of corn across the width of the pan, securing them so they are suspended above the bottom of the pan. Bake for 1 hour. Remove the corn from the foil and enjoy while steaming hot. Serves 6.

Great Aunt Rose's Chicken

Served with crusty French bread, this casserole is a complete meal. Kim Mowder's great aunt created the recipe just after the invention of Velveeta and Kim's mother asked for it each time she visited Aunt Rose in Baytown, Texas.

1 whole chicken
2 tablespoons butter
1 cup chopped celery
1 medium bell pepper, chopped
1 large onion, chopped
1/2 cup sliced fresh mushrooms
1/4 cup chopped pimento
4 cups cooked egg noodles
1/2 pound Velveeta, cubed
1/2 cup whole milk

In a large pot of salted water over medium-low heat, poach the chicken until the meat starts to fall from the bone, about 1 hour. Remove the chicken and cool, reserving the broth to cook the egg noodles. Remove the bones and skin and shred the chicken; set aside. In a large skillet over medium heat, melt the butter and sauté the celery, pepper, onion and mushrooms until softened. Add the pimento and chicken and remove from the heat. Stir in the noodles and Velveeta and pour the mixture into a large buttered baking dish. Pour over the milk and bake, covered, at 300 degrees for 1 hour. Remove from the oven, correct the seasoning and enjoy. Serves 6.

THE BISHOP'S HAT HOUSE

You'll find a sweet secret in this eye-catching, turreted Third Street mansion locals call the Bishop's Hat House. It's the Old Louisville Candy Company, where Ron and Jane Harris make Happy Balls, a confectionery creation named in honor of Ron's Aunt Happy, the lady who passed down the original recipe. Retired actors, Ron and Jane started the company in 2005 after they relocated to Kentucky from New York City; since then their star product has become the city's favorite bourbon candy.

When they're not busy hand-dipping bourbon balls and shipping them to eager customers around the country, Ron and Jane enjoy spending time reading in front of the fire in their cherry-paneled library. In all, there are nine fireplaces and more than a dozen rooms in the spacious residence, where original hardwood floors and elegant millwork abounds. The redbrick dwelling, built in 1894 for tobacco man John C. Middleton, has a cozy kitchen where the Harris's cook up a wide variety of dishes. A favorite meal is this easy brisket recipe with green beans and spoon bread, which pays homage both to the Jewish heritage on Jane's side of the family and Ron's Kentucky roots.

Architectural Note: A turret (from Latin *turris*) is a small tower that projects vertically from the wall of a structure.

Nana's Brisket with Sweet Green Beans

Hours of slow cooking give this humble cut of beef the melt-in-your-mouth consistency that will make it a family favorite at your house.

2 tablespoons olive oil
5 carrots, finely chopped
1 large yellow onion,
   finely chopped
2 large cloves garlic, minced
1 beef brisket (4 pounds)
1 packet onion soup mix
2 1/2 cups water

In a large Dutch oven over medium heat, add the olive oil and sauté the carrots, onion and garlic until the onions are translucent, about 5 minutes. Remove vegetables from the pan and set aside; turn up the heat and brown brisket well on all sides in the Dutch oven; return the vegetables to the pan with the brisket, add soup mix and water and bake, covered, at 325 degrees for 3 hours or until fork-tender.

For the Sweet Green Beans, cover 1 pound of fresh green beans with water in a saucepan, add 1/2 cup brown sugar and 1/2 teaspoon kosher salt, and cook over medium heat until tender. In a skillet over medium-low heat, melt 2 tablespoons salted butter and whisk in 2 tablespoons all-purpose flour. Turn up the heat and add 1/2 cup of liquid from the brisket, stirring constantly; when the mixture starts to boil, add to the beans and stir to combine. Serve with the sliced brisket and enjoy. Serves 6.

Ron's Kentucky Spoon Bread

This southern-inspired soufflé is both fluffy and flavorful. Ron recommends topping with a dab of fresh butter before serving.

2 cups whole milk
1 cup extra-fine cornmeal
4 eggs, separated
1 tablespoon sugar
3/4 teaspoon salt
4 tablespoons salted butter, plus extra

In a double boiler over medium heat warm the milk until bubbles form around the edges. Sprinkle in the cornmeal and mix well, stirring constantly. Add the 4 egg yolks, one at a time, followed by the sugar, salt and 4 tablespoons of butter. Beat the egg whites until stiff and fold into the mixture. Bake in a buttered casserole or soufflé dish in a 325-degree oven for about 45 minutes or until risen and golden brown. Serve immediately. Serves 6.

To get your own Happy Balls, contact:

Old Louisville Candy Company
1390 South Third Street
Louisville, Kentucky 40208
(502) 637-2227

CARSON HOUSE

In Old Louisville, Garvin Place is known as a secluded side street that intersects the busy business corridor of West Oak Street. Originally a stretch of Fifth Street, it was renamed Garvin Place in the 1880s, most likely in honor of William Garvin, a successful businessman who died during a steamboat accident on the Ohio River in 1868. Many of the homes found there today date to the latter part of the 1800s, and one of these is the house occupied by Bob and Norma Laufer. The Laufers have spent more than 20 years restoring and remodeling their brick dwelling, which dates to the mid 1870s, and over the years they've converted it back to a comfortable single-family residence. In the process they've preserved a piece of local history, all the while uncovering interesting snippets about the home's past and previous occupants.

The very first resident was a plumber by the name of J.M. Carson, and in the very early 1900s it was home to the Cremin family and their Vita Company, a manufacturer of proprietary medicines. The Laufers are very active in the neighborhood today, and Norma is a regular volunteer at the Visitors Center in Historic Old Louisville. When they entertain, the two recipes that follow are favorites among their guests.

34

Creamy Corn Pudding

12 ounces frozen corn, thawed
15-ounce can creamed corn
8 tablespoons all-purpose flour
1 teaspoon kosher salt
4 heaping teaspoons sugar
4 tablespoons melted butter
4 large eggs, beaten
2 cups whole milk
1 cup half-and-half
1/2 cup Parmesan cheese

Norma says this tasty side dish has a custard-like consistency and wonderful mouth feel. "It is the most asked-for dish by my grown children and is served at every holiday and birthday celebrations, even in the summer."

In a large mixing bowl, stir together the corn, the creamed corn, flour, salt, sugar and butter. Whisk eggs with the milk and half-and-half and stir into the corn mixture. Pour into a large baking dish that has been sprayed with vegetable oil and bake at 450 degrees for about 45 minutes. Stir with a long-pronged fork several times during baking; during the last 10 minutes of baking, sprinkle grated Parmesan cheese on top. Serves 8.

36

Bouef Bourguignon

According to Norma, this classic French stew tastes even better the day after, so it's always a good idea to make enough for leftovers.

1 tablespoon olive oil
8 ounces bacon, diced
1 1/2 pounds beef chuck,
    cut into 1-inch pieces
1 pound baby carrots
2 yellow onions, chopped
1 tablespoon kosher salt
2 teaspoons black pepper
2 teaspoons minced garlic
1/2 cup brandy
1 bottle dry red wine
2 1/2 cups beef stock
1 tablespoon tomato paste
1 teaspoon fresh thyme leaves
4 tablespoons unsalted butter,
    at room temperature
3 tablespoons all-purpose flour
1 pound frozen pearl onions, thawed
1 pound button mushrooms, thickly sliced

Preheat the oven to 250 degrees. Heat olive oil in a large Dutch oven over medium heat and add the bacon; cook until the bacon is lightly browned. Remove the bacon with a slotted spoon to a large plate. Pat the beef cubes dry and sprinkle with salt and pepper. Sear the beef in the hot oil for 5 minutes, turning to brown on all sides. Remove beef to the plate with the bacon and set aside. Add the carrots, chopped onions, salt and pepper to the pan and cook for 10 minutes, stirring occasionally. Add garlic and cook for 1 minute before pouring in the brandy and returning the meat and bacon to the pot with any juices on the plate. Add the wine, beef stock, tomato paste and thyme and bring to a boil. Cover and bake for 1 1/4 hours, or until meat and vegetables are tender. Remove from oven and place on top of the stove.

Use a fork to combine 2 tablespoons of the butter with the flour and stir into the stew, along with the onions. In a pan, brown the mushrooms in the remaining 2 tablespoons of butter and add to the stew. Bring to a boil, reduce the heat and simmer for 15 minutes. Correct the seasoning and serve with toasted slices of country bread. Serves 6-8.

THE CONRAD-CALDWELL HOUSE

In a neighborhood known for its stunning Victorian architecture and grand mansions, there are several residences that stand out for their sheer size and lavish details. One of them – perhaps the grandest of them all – is the lovely Conrad-Caldwell House on St. James Court. Built between 1892 and 1895 for Theophilus Conrad, an Alsatian immigrant who made his fortune in the leather tanning industry, this imposing structure arose as the epitome of opulence and hospitality in Gilded Age Old Louisville. More than a century later, this grandeur lives on, the bygone of an era that has been preserved for all to enjoy at the only historic house museum in the neighborhood.

Among the many supporters of the museum today are Margaret and Robert Young – and if they seem a bit more interested than most in its preservation and upkeep, that's because the beautiful old mansion figures prominently in their family tree. Margaret's great-grandparents, William and Elaine Caldwell, called it home after purchasing it from the widow of Theophilus Conrad after his death in 1905, and the imposing limestone residence would remain in the Caldwell family for the next three and a half decades.

Margaret, their great-granddaughter, sits on the museum's board of directors today, keeping alive her family's involvement with this, one of the most venerable homes in the Commonwealth. Not only does Margaret volunteer her time to promote the house during neighborhood events such as the annual Spirit Ball, she also regularly shares her family's history with visitors who arrive to tour the mansion. Among the many highlights are elaborate quilt-patterned hardwood floors in each of the rooms and a grand stairway with hand-carved fleur-de-lis and stunning stained glass windows.

The Conrad-Caldwell House offers regular tours and is available for rentals. For more information, contact them at:

Conrad-Caldwell House Museum
1402 St. James Court
Louisville, Kentucky 40208
(502) 636-5023

Gingerbread with Lemon Sauce

A cherished family recipe, this easy spice cake was a favorite of Walter Caldwell, the son of William and Elaine Caldwell. A drizzle of lemon sauce adds a tangy twist to this Victorian favorite.

1 cup granulated sugar
1 heaping tablespoon butter
1 cup molasses
1 large egg
1 heaping teaspoon baking soda
1 cup buttermilk
3 cups all-purpose flour
1 teaspoon ground ginger
1 teaspoon cinnamon
1/2 teaspoon allspice

Lemon Sauce

1/2 cup granulated sugar
1 tablespoon cornstarch
1 cup boiling water
2 tablespoons butter
1 tablespoon lemon zest
3 tablespoons lemon juice
1/8 teaspoon salt

Preheat the oven to 350 degrees. In a large bowl of a stand mixer, cream together the sugar, butter, molasses and egg. Stir the soda into the buttermilk to activate and set aside. In a medium bowl sift together the flour, ginger, cinnamon and allspice. To the creamed mixture, alternately add thirds of the dry ingredients and half of the buttermilk starting and ending with the flour. Beat on high until the lumps disappear, but be careful not to overbeat. Pour into a greased and floured 9-by 9-inch pan for 45 minutes, or until a toothpick inserted in the center comes out clean. For the Lemon Sauce, combine sugar, cornstarch and water in a small saucepan over medium heat and bring to a boil. Cook slowly, stirring constantly until thick and clear. Remove from the heat and whisk in the butter, lemon zest, juice and salt. Spoon over warm gingerbread and enjoy. Serves 9.

About the Architect

Born January 28, 1858, Arthur Loomis relocated to Jeffersonville, Indiana, from Massachusetts with his family just before the start of the Civil War; around 1910 he moved to Louisville. After working several years for noted architect Charles J. Clarke the two became partners in 1891 and created one of Louisville's most prestigious architectural firms. After Clarke's death in 1908, Loomis primarily worked alone and produced some of his most noted works, including the Carnegie Library in Jeffersonville, Indiana and the J.B. Speed Art Museum. Many of his earlier works, such as the Conrad-Caldwell House, show a preference for the rounded arches and rough-hewn stone typical of the Richardsonian Romanesque style.

Hattie Dick's Cranberries

In the late 1800s Hattie Cochran was immortalized as *The Little Colonel* in the books of Annie Fellows Johnston. In 1912 she married Albert Conrad Dick, the grandson of Theopholis and Mary Conrad, the original owners of the lovely mansion at 1402 St. James Court. Since Albert had lived next door to the Caldwells when they lived on Second Street, he and Hattie remained lifelong friends of the Caldwells. This simple recipe for cranberries is still a year-round favorite with Margaret's family today.

1 quart cranberries
1 pint sugar
1/2 pint water

In a large saucepan over medium-high heat, boil the cranberries, sugar and water for 12 minutes. Remove from the heat and strain prior to serving. Serves 8.

41

CONRAD'S FOLLY

Old Louisville is a neighborhood known for its stunning mansions, stylish town homes and comfortable single-family residences, however there is a variety of elegant apartments and condominiums as well. One of them is the St. James Flats, believed to be the first apartment building in the neighborhood. Constructed by Theophilus Conrad in 1897 as an investment property, the building sparked a controversy with its St. James Court neighbors, many of whom objected to a multi-storied building towering over their graceful boulevard. When the case went to court, Mr. Conrad eventually prevailed, but the residents of St. James Court refused to accept the eyesore. The dispute came to a fiery resolution in 1912, when a mysterious blaze destroyed the top stories, leaving a three-storied structure with ten beautiful units in its wake.

Todd McGill and Keith Simon chose to make their home in a third-floor space with a balcony that affords panoramic views of Central Park and nearby perennial gardens. Although the beautifully restored condominium has original features such as gleaming hardwood floors and inviting fireplaces, the décor is smart and contemporary – no doubt the result of the owners' penchant for design.

Pappy's Sweet & Sour Bourbon Meatballs

In Kentucky, bourbon flavors life and food. This appetizer named after one of The Flats most famous residents, Pappy van Winkle, is a favorite at parties. According to Todd and Keith, guests often linger beside the chafing dish so they can eat more than their share of these tasty meatballs.

1 1/2 pounds lean ground beef
1 1/2 cups bread crumbs
1/4 cup finely chopped onion
1 teaspoon kosher salt
1/2 teaspoon black pepper
2 tablespoons
   whole-grain mustard
1 large egg
12-ounce jar orange marmalade
1/2 cup chili sauce
1/4 cup bourbon
1/4 teaspoon hot sauce

Preheat the oven to 400 degrees. In a large bowl, combine the ground beef, bread crumbs, onion, salt, pepper, mustard and egg. Mix well. Use your hands to form 1 1/4-inch meatballs and place in an ungreased baking pan; bake for 20 minutes. In a large saucepan over low heat, stir together the marmalade, chili sauce, bourbon and hot sauce and simmer for 15 minutes, stirring frequently. Add the meatballs to the sauce and stir to coat. Garnish with sprigs of fresh mint. Makes about 40 meatballs.

Bourbon Mint Punch

A family recipe adapted from the traditional mint julep, this bourbon and mint punch sparkles with the addition of pineapple juice and ginger ale. Todd says Pappy van Winkle would've preferred his whiskey straight up but guests agree it's even better as the star ingredient in this summery punch when enjoyed on the balcony.

1 quart cranberry juice
1 quart pineapple juice
1 cup orange juice
1/2 cup lemon juice
1 cup bourbon
Two 12-ounce bottles
   ginger ale, chilled
4 mint leaves, torn

In a large punch bowl, combine the cranberry juice, pineapple juice, orange juice, lemon juice and bourbon. Refrigerate until well chilled and add the ginger ale and mint immediately before serving. Makes 20 servings.

45

THE DUPONT MANSION

For information about the DuPont Mansion, contact them at:

DuPont Mansion Bed & Breakfast
1317 South Fourth Street
Louisville, Kentucky 40208
(502) 638.0045
info@oldlouisvilleinns.com

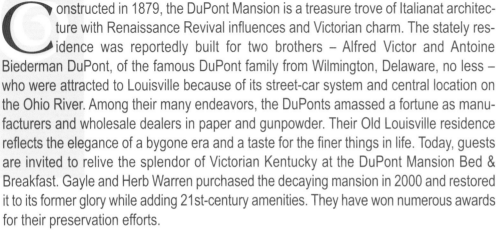

Constructed in 1879, the DuPont Mansion is a treasure trove of Italianat architecture with Renaissance Revival influences and Victorian charm. The stately residence was reportedly built for two brothers – Alfred Victor and Antoine Biederman DuPont, of the famous DuPont family from Wilmington, Delaware, no less – who were attracted to Louisville because of its street-car system and central location on the Ohio River. Among their many endeavors, the DuPonts amassed a fortune as manufacturers and wholesale dealers in paper and gunpowder. Their Old Louisville residence reflects the elegance of a bygone era and a taste for the finer things in life. Today, guests are invited to relive the splendor of Victorian Kentucky at the DuPont Mansion Bed & Breakfast. Gayle and Herb Warren purchased the decaying mansion in 2000 and restored it to its former glory while adding 21st-century amenities. They have won numerous awards for their preservation efforts.

Chocolate Velvet Pound Cake

The word "velvet" is no exaggeration for this long-time favorite of innkeeper, Jane Allen. Smooth on the palate, this pound cake is enhanced by a satiny glaze of chocolate ganache.

1 1/2 cups semisweet chocolate morsels
1/2 cup butter, softened
16-ounce package light brown sugar
3 large eggs
2 cups all-purpose flour
1 teaspoon baking soda
1/2 teaspoon salt
1 cup sour cream
1 cup hot water
2 teaspoons vanilla extract
1/4 cup powdered sugar

Melt chocolate morsels in a bowl, in the microwave, at 30 second intervals. Stir melted chocolate until smooth. In a separate bowl, beat butter and brown sugar at medium speed for five minutes. Add eggs to brown sugar-butter mixture, one-at-a-time, beating until just blended. Add melted chocolate, and beat until smooth. Sift together the flour, baking soda and salt. Beginning and ending with the flour mixture, gradually add the sifted dry ingredients to the chocolate mixture, alternating with sour cream, and beat at low speed until blended. Continue mixing at low speed and slowly pour in hot water in a slow and steady stream, until just blended. Stir in vanilla extract and pour batter into a greased and floured 10-inch tube pan. Bake at 350 degrees for 60 minutes, or until a long wooden pick inserted in the center comes out clean. Cool in the pan, on a wire rack, for 15 minutes. Remove from pan and let the cake cool completely, before sifting powered sugar on the top of the cake. Garnish with a dipped strawberry and serve with warm chocolate ganache. Serves 12.

Chocolate Ganache

1/2 cup whipping cream
12 ounces semisweet chocolate morsels
3 tablespoons butter

Heat the whipping cream in a saucepan until bubbles start to form around the edges. Place the chocolate in a large mixing bowl and pour the hot cream over the morsels; let sit for 2 minutes. Whisk together until the chocolate melts and the mixture is free of lumps. Add the butter and beat at medium speed until smooth and satiny.

Italian Cream Cake

This recipe is a staple for DuPont Mansion innkeeper Jane Allen, who has served it to family and guests for 50 years. Moist and satisfying, it is a favorite with overnighters at the elegant bed and breakfast inn, where complimentary desserts are served every afternoon.

1 stick butter, softened
1/2 cup vegetable oil
2 cups sugar
5 large eggs, separated
2 cups all-purpose flour
1 teaspoon baking soda
1 teaspoon baking powder
1 cup buttermilk
1 teaspoon vanilla extract
3 1/2 ounces flaked coconut
1/2 cup chopped pecans

In a large mixing bowl, cream softened butter with oil and sugar. Add egg yolks, one at a time, and beat well. Sift flour with soda and baking powder and add half of the flour mixture and to the creamed mixture with half of the buttermilk. Mix to combine and add the remaining flour and buttermilk; beat at medium speed for 2 minutes or until smooth. Stir in vanilla extract, coconut, and nuts. Beat egg whites until stiff and fold the beaten egg whites into batter. Pour into three 8-inch pans that have been greased and floured. Bake at 350 degrees for 25 to 30 minutes, or until a pick inserted in the center comes out clean. Cool for five minutes in pans on a wire rack, before inverting the pans and allowing the cakes to cook completely.

Cream Cheese Frosting

8 ounces cream cheese
3 cups powdered sugar
1 teaspoon vanilla extract
1/2 cup chopped pecans

While the cake layers cool, use a hand mixer to blend the cream cheese, powdered sugar, and vanilla extract until smooth. When the cakes have cooled completely, place one layer on a plate and brush away any crumbs; spread about ¼ of the frosting on the surface and top with another layer. Repeat the process to use the third cake. Spread the remaining frosting on the top and sides of the cake and sprinkle with chopped pecans. Serves 12.

THE FERGUSON MANSION
The Filson Historical Society

Completed in 1905 at a reported cost of $100,000, this graceful structure at 1310 South Third Street is often cited as the most elegant mansion in the city. Designed by the architectural firm of Dodd and Cobb for industrialist Edwin Hite Ferguson, it's a beautiful example of Beaux Arts architecture that showcased the Ferguson's success and social status in the neighborhood.

Imposing in size, the Ferguson Mansion boasts a mansard roof and a symmetrical façade embellished with garlands, floral patterns, and oval cartouches – all details that make it one of the most visually engaging residences in the region. On the interior, additional details such as hand-painted murals, Tiffany light fixtures, art-glass wall sconces and stunning woodwork round out the appeal of this grand home.

In 1986 the Ferguson Mansion became the headquarters for the Filson Historical Society, a prestigious regional organization with roots that go back to 1884. During the day, visitors are welcome to stop by and enjoy the public rooms on the ground floor and discover for themselves why this is an Old Louisville treasure.

Benedictine

One of the most famous figures to emerge from Kentucky kitchens was Jennie Benedict, an Old Louisville restaurateur who often catered parties for the Fergusons. Known for her wonderful cakes and tea sandwiches, she concocted a special cream cheese-and-cucumber spread that still lives on today. Although it's most often used as a filling for sandwiches, it also makes a great dip for vegetables and crackers.

1 large English cucumber,
   coarsely chopped
2 tablespoons chopped
   white onion
1/4 cup chopped fresh parsley
1/4 cup mayonnaise
16 ounces cream cheese,
   softened
1 teaspoon kosher salt
1/2 teaspoon ground white pepper

In a food processor, purée the cucumber, skin and all, with the onion. Remove from the processor and use a clean towel or a bit of cheesecloth to squeeze all the liquid out of the mixture that you can. Set aside. In the food processor purée the parsley and mayonnaise to form a smooth paste. This will give the Benedictine its characteristically green color without using food coloring. Add the cream cheese to the processor and pulse until smooth. Transfer to the bowl with the onion-cucumber mix, season with the salt and pepper, and combine thoroughly. Refrigerate for at least an hour and enjoy with celery and pretzel sticks.

Pimento Cheese

Easy to prepare, pimento cheese is a staple that has come to be identified with southern cuisine. As a filling for sandwiches or a dip for raw vegetables, pimento cheese is the perfect snack or party food at any time of year.

2 pounds extra sharp
   Cheddar cheese
1 1/4 cups mayonnaise
1 1/2 cups finely diced roasted
   red peppers
1/2 teaspoon kosher salt
1/2 teaspoon ground white pepper

Grate the cheese into a large mixing bowl; add the mayonnaise, chopped red peppers, salt and white pepper and combine. Refrigerate for at least two hours to allow the flavors to meld. Serve with crackers and slices of toasted rye bread. Makes about 4 cups.

What is a mansion?

For most, a mansion is a very large and highly decorated dwelling, but beyond that no formal definition exists for the word. Usually the home of a wealthy person or family, a mansion is also designed to show hospitality and flaunt a degree of social status. In this country, most realtors define a mansion as a residence of over 7,000 or 8,000 square feet, however in Europe and early America traditional mansions contained a ballroom and numerous bedrooms.

Orlando Gianni, a noted figure in Prairie School architecture, designed the glass-tile fireplace surround in the Ferguson Mansion dining room.

52

53

THE HARRY LUCAS HOUSE

In the early 1890s, after Louisville's famed Southern Exposition building was dismantled and removed, local pharmaceutical salesman Harry V. Lucas purchased land from the Victoria Land Grant Company and began construction on an impressive Richardsonian Romanesque mansion. The three-story structure has a façade of rusticated stone and a tower feature at the northeast corner. A single-story, fully rounded bay dominates the lower level of the home, while the roofline is highlighted by a gable with stone pediment and a majestic turret with scalloped slate shingling. Mr. Lucas sold the property to W.H. May in 1895, and he lived there with his family until the early 1900s when it became home to Hiram P. Roberts, the secretary and treasurer of the Mengel Box Company. Today, it is home to Doug Keller, whose recent renovations have turned the elegant home into a stylish showcase of Old-World charm and modern convenience. In addition to a comfortable theater room in the carriage house, the residence includes a landscaped rear courtyard with a stone martini bar, features that have earned Doug the reputation as one of the neighborhood's best hosts.

Hearty Bean Soup

Doug likes to entertain and when he cooks, he cooks a lot. If you don't manage to finish off this pot of soup, don't worry – it freezes well.

Bean Soup

An old family recipe, this hearty dish uses a variety of dried beans to embellish the main flavoring ingredient – country ham. As with most comfort-food recipes, one can be creative with the ingredients here.

2 cups great northern beans
2 cups navy beans
**1 pound country ham,
    cut into large chunks**
**1 pound sugar-cured ham,
    finely chopped**
2 large onions, chopped
4 stalks celery, chopped
8 cups tomato juice

Rinse the beans and soak for at least 3 hours in warm water. Strain and add the beans to a large stock pot with the country ham, the sugar-cured ham, onions, celery and tomato juice. Cook, covered, for at least 1 hour over medium heat, adding water if necessary. When the beans are tender, correct the seasoning and enjoy with warm cornbread. Serves 8.

Stewed Meatloaf

A long-time favorite with Doug's family and friends, this one-pot meal is quick, easy and delicious.

1 1/2 pounds ground beef
1 cup bread crumbs
2 medium onions, chopped
1 large egg, beaten
1 teaspoon salt
1/2 teaspoon ground
   black pepper
2 cloves garlic, minced
1/2 cup chopped parsley
2 cups tomato sauce
2 cups tomato juice
4 large red potatoes,
   peeled and quartered
4 carrots, cut into chunks
1 tablespoon
   Worcestershire sauce
1/2 cup ketchup

In a large bowl, combine the ground beef, bread crumbs, onions, egg, salt, pepper, garlic and parsley. Shape into a loaf and place in an electric skillet on 200 degrees and cook, covered, for 20 minutes. Drain excess liquid from the skillet and add the tomato sauce, tomato juice, potatoes and carrots. Sprinkle the Worcestershire sauce over the meatloaf and spread ketchup over the surface. Cover and simmer for about 1 hour, adding extra tomato juice as needed. Correct the seasoning and enjoy. Serves 6.

THE HENRIETTA ORMSBY HOUSE

This comfortable residence was one of three built side by side on the same block of Sixth Street for Henrietta Ormsby in 1899. The eight-room dwelling has four working fireplaces, original hardwood flooring and leaded stained glass windows, as well as a New Orleans-inspired courtyard with six fountains and a Koi pond. It's no surprise that this, the home of Howard and Jena Rosenberg, has been featured on Old Louisville's yearly Hidden Treasures Garden Tour. The interior of the house blends a lifetime of acquisitions of the owners, mature newlyweds whose passion for Old Louisville is borne-out by a complete framed collection of posters from the St. James Court Art Show. Merging with the home's Victorian details are her collection of Art Deco pieces, his collection of Jewish art, and their collection of Mardis Gras memorabilia. The result is a vibrant and eclectic melding of styles, including an ultra-modern black granite kitchen that leads conveniently to the courtyard garden.

Garvin Gate Gumbo

The Rosenbergs have named this popular dish after the Garvin Gate Blues Festival, an annual fall event in Old Louisville – and the largest free neighborhood street music festival in the city. Given their many trips to the Big Easy and the time they've spent sampling the city's food and music, Howard and Jena know their blues and gumbo.

1 whole chicken, cut into pieces
5 tablespoons olive oil
1 1/2 pounds andouille sausage, sliced
6 tablespoons all-purpose flour
2 large onions, chopped
1 green pepper, chopped
2 stalks celery, finely diced
2 1/2 quarts chicken broth
3 cloves garlic, minced
3 bay leaves
1/2 teaspoon thyme
1/2 teaspoon basil
1/4 teaspoon cayenne pepper
1/4 teaspoon allspice
Salt and pepper to taste
Chopped green onions
Filé powder

In a heavy pot or Dutch oven over medium-high heat, brown the chicken in the olive oil. Place sausage in the pot with the chicken, and brown for 5 minutes; remove the chicken and sausage and set aside. Reduce the heat to medium and add the flour to the oil in the pot; stirring constantly, cook until brown in color. Add chopped onion, green pepper, and celery to the roux and sauté until tender. Add the chicken broth, garlic, bay leaves, thyme, basil, cayenne, allspice, salt and pepper; simmer for 45 minutes. Return the chicken and sausage to the pot and cook until the chicken is tender, about 30 minutes. Add green onions and remove from heat. Let sit 15 minutes and then serve with a spoon of steamed white rice. Add a pinch of filé powder to each serving of gumbo and serve with crusty baguettes. Serves 8.

Scalloped Apples

This simple dish is a favorite with Howard and Jena's guests. It's so versatile that it can be served as either a side or a dessert.

2 sticks butter
1 1/2 cups sugar
1 1/2 cups self-rising flour
1 pound Velveeta cheese, diced
Two 18-ounce cans sliced apples

In a large mixing bowl, cream the butter and sugar; stir in the flour and cheese to mix well. Drain the apples and layer in the bottom of a greased 9-by 13-inch baking dish. Spread the cheese mixture on top and bake at 350 degrees for 30 minutes, or until the top is golden brown. Serves 6.

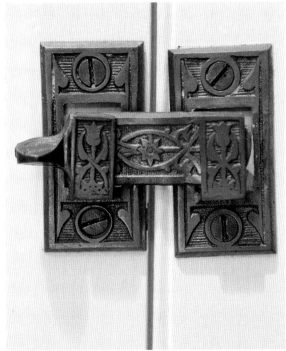

JOHN DEPPEN RESIDENCE

U nder the slate-roofed cupola of this three-story home on South Second Street, is a residence that synergizes original details with modern amenities. Although the house has benefited from extensive remodeling since the beginning of the preservation movement in Old Louisville, the result is refreshingly true to its Victorian origins. In addition to the huge pocket doors and original leaded stained glass windows throughout, the residence has an inviting stairwell that has been the site of prom pictures and wedding photos for the daughters of Marry Morrow, the current owner.

There are also crystal chandeliers, an iron claw-foot bathtub, nine working fireplaces and a library with a floor-to-ceiling bookcase brimming with world literature and antique books. Built around 1890 for John Deppen, the house exudes a dramatic Victorian décor today, with deep reds, greens, plum and wine colors and various antiques Mary has refinished herself.

Rooms in Mary's house are cozy and lead one-to-the-other in a way that offers a surprise at each turn. For example, the stack of hatboxes in the master bedroom sitting area looks like part of the décor, until you discover that Mary is an official host to thoroughbred owners during the annual Kentucky Derby. Her most frequent guests were Bob and Beverly Lewis - whose Silver Charm and Charismatic won the Derby in 1997 and 1999.

Bourbon Slush

Mary loves serving this icy citrus-sweet bourbon concoction to her guests because it's simple to prepare and it stores well in the freezer. Although it's a natural in the warmer months when her friends and family can be found wandering among the tall roses in the carefully tended courtyard garden, one can imagine enjoying this treat in front of the iron-faced hearth in the kitchen or tucked away in an overstuffed chair in the library.

7 cups water
2 cups bourbon
7 tablespoons instant iced tea
2 cups sugar
12 ounces frozen orange juice concentrate, thawed
12 ounces frozen lemonade concentrate, thawed
6 ounces frozen limeade concentrate, thawed

To prepare the slush, pour the water and bourbon into a resealable Rubbermaid-type container and add the instant tea. Stir in the sugar, orange juice, lemonade and limeade concentrates and mix well. Freeze, covered, for 48 hours. To serve, scoop into a tall glass with a generous splash of ginger ale; or enjoy on its own like an Italian granita. Makes about 24 drinks.

Not Exactly Derby Pie

Created at Kern's Bakery in the 1950s, the original Derby Pie is registered with the U.S. Patent Office. Its hallmark ingredients are walnuts and chocolate, but imitations often include pecans, bourbon, or caramel. Recipes for homemade versions of this Derby-time favorite abound, and a favorite is this easy-to-prepare reproduction enjoyed by Mary throughout the year.

1/2 cup butter
1 cup sugar
2 eggs, beaten
1/2 cup all-purpose flour
1 teaspoon vanilla extract
6 ounces semisweet chocolate chips
1 cup chopped pecans
9-inch unbaked pie shell

Preheat the oven to 325 degrees. Melt the butter in a glass bowl in the microwave. Whisk in the sugar, eggs, flour and vanilla extract. Spread the chocolate chips and pecans over the bottom of the unbaked pie shell. Pour the egg mixture over the chocolate chips and nuts and bake approximately 1 hour or until the pie appears slightly firm when removed from the oven. Serve warm or at room temperature with whipped cream or vanilla ice cream. Serves 6.

THE J.B. SPEED MANSION

This sprawling mansion on Ormsby Avenue was built in 1883, the same year Louisville's famous Southern Exposition opened. Its builder and first resident was prominent contractor, Dexter Belknap, who is believed to have built the Louisville and Portland Canal in 1830. Though Belknap's accomplishments were significant, the house is named after its most famous resident, James Breckenridge Speed.

It was Speed's second wife, Hattie Bishop Speed, however, whose presence would become immortal. "Miss Hattie" occupied the house after J.B. Speed's death in 1912 and gained fame for establishing the Speed Art Museum. Known for her love of music, she had Arthur Loomis add a music room furnished with a Steinway grand piano and an Aeolian-Skinner pipe-organ to the house in 1915; to enhance acoustics, the noted architect used wood pulp in the walls and battleship linoleum on the floor. Long after her passing in the 1940s, many local residents still remember Hattie for her generosity and weekly musical soirees.

The music room is now a stunning library for the mansion's current occupants – the attorneys of the law firm of Franklin, Gray and White. And although it has been adapted for commercial use, Larry and Judy Franklin made sure to preserve much of the original charm of the rambling 48-room residence when they acquired the property in the 1980s. Public areas such as the study and front parlor are much as they would have been in Hattie's day, and although the dining room, elegant as ever, isn't used for formal repasts anymore, the Franklins have kept alive Hattie's penchant for entertaining. Much-anticipated company parties give Judy the opportunity to show off her skills in the kitchen with a variety of recipes. Favorites include the following, named for the Franklin's five grandchildren.

Haleigh's Beef Tenderloin with Olive Relish

5-pound beef tenderloin,
  trimmed and tied every 3 inches
2 teaspoons kosher salt
2 tablespoons extra-virgin olive oil
2 tablespoons cracked
  black pepper
2 large garlic cloves, peeled
1/4 teaspoon salt
2 tablespoons Dijon mustard
1/2 cup fresh lemon juice
1/2 cup extra-virgin olive oil
3 cups pitted black olives, drained
2 cups pitted green olives, drained

Sprinkle entire surface of beef tenderloin with kosher salt and place on a rack over large rimmed baking sheet; refrigerate, uncovered, for at least 36 hours. One hour before roasting, remove beef from the refrigerator and let stand at room temperature. Rub the tenderloin with 2 tablespoons olive oil and sprinkle with cracked pepper, pressing to adhere. Roast for about 30 minutes in a 425-degree oven, or until an instant-read thermometer inserted into thickest part of the meat registers 125°F (for medium-rare). Remove from the oven and let rest 15 minutes. To prepare the olive relish, place the garlic, 1/4 teaspoon salt, mustard, lemon juice, 1/2 cup olive oil, black and green olives in a food processor, and pulse to coarsely chop the olives. Serve at room temperature as an accompaniment to sliced beef tenderloin. Serves 8.

Spencer's Caesar Salad

2 anchovy fillets, drained
1 teaspoon minced garlic
1/2 teaspoon kosher salt
1/2 teaspoon black pepper
1 large egg, at room temperature
2 tablespoons freshly grated Parmesan cheese
1 tablespoon fresh lemon juice
1 teaspoon Dijon mustard
1/4 cup extra-virgin olive oil
1 teaspoon Worcestershire sauce
1/2 teaspoon hot sauce
4 hearts romaine, torn into pieces

In a small bowl, use a fork to mash together the anchovies, garlic, salt and pepper. Add the egg to the mixture and whisk; whisk in the Parmesan cheese, lemon juice and mustard. Drizzle in the olive oil in a steady stream, whisking constantly to form a thick emulsion. Add the Worcestershire and hot sauce, and toss with the lettuce. Divide among four large salad plates and top with additional Parmesan cheese and croutons if desired. Serves 4.

Juels' and Laihl's Banana Bread

1/2 cup vegetable oil
1 1/2 cups sugar
2 eggs, well beaten
1/4 teaspoon salt
1 1/2 cups sifted all-purpose flour
1 teaspoon baking soda
1/3 cup buttermilk
4 ripe bananas, mashed

Preheat oven to 350 degrees. Grease 2 regular-size loaf pans. In a large bowl, cream the oil, sugar and eggs together; add the salt, flour, baking soda, buttermilk and bananas and stir to combine. Divide the batter equally between the pans and bake for 45 minutes, or until a toothpick inserted in the center comes out clean. Serves 8.

Zane's Favorite Spaghetti and Meatballs

2 cloves garlic, minced
1 large onion, chopped
3 tablespoons olive oil
1/2 cup tomato paste
1 cup tomato sauce
2 cups diced tomatoes
2 cups fresh sliced mushrooms
2 teaspoons sugar
2 cups water
1/4 cup chopped parsley
1 1/2 teaspoons chopped fresh rosemary
1 1/2 teaspoons chopped fresh basil
1 1/2 teaspoons chopped fresh thyme
1 1/2 teaspoons chopped fresh oregano
1/2 teaspoon pepper
1 bay leaf
1 1/2 pounds ground chuck
2 tablespoons chopped onion
1/2 cup bread crumbs
1/4 cup milk
1 egg
1/2 teaspoon salt
1/2 teaspoon pepper
1 clove garlic, minced
1/4 cup grated Parmesan cheese

In a large saucepan over medium heat, sauté the 2 cloves garlic and onion in the olive oil until golden brown. Add the tomato paste, tomato sauce, tomatoes, mushrooms, sugar, water, parsley, rosemary, basil, thyme, oregano, pepper and bay leaf and simmer, covered, for at least 2 hours. Prepare the meatballs by mixing together the ground chuck with the 2 tablespoons onion, bread crumbs, milk, egg, salt, pepper, garlic and Parmesan cheese. Shape the mixture into balls and brown in a large skillet over medium heat; drain off fat and add meatballs to tomato sauce. Simmer for another 30 minutes. Serve over spaghetti, prepared according to package instructions. Serves 6

THE J.P. REHM HOUSE

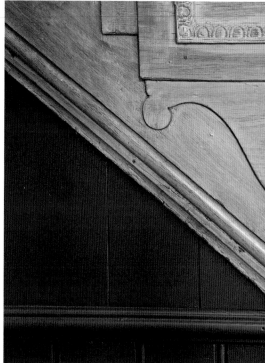

This Neoclassical home was built in 1904 for J.P. Rehm, an engineer with the Louisville & Nashville Railroad. One of the newest constructions on South Sixth Street, the two-bayed brick home has a classical front porch with dentils and decorative wrought iron detailing that is repeated in the fence railing. A large gabled dormer with Palladian-inspired windows affords grand views of the changing landscape of Central Park, which sits across the street. In fact, the J.P. Rehm house was erected the same year Louisville acquired the park and engaged the firm of Frederick Law Olmstead to create its new design.

More than a century later, original woodwork greets visitors in the foyer, which is illuminated by period light fixtures. Although owners Mike and Candace Milligan have modernized parts of the residence, they have managed to maintain much of its historical integrity. Among recent changes, the Milligans added a three-car garage and a modern kitchen with stainless steel and granite countertops. There is also a formal backyard garden and walled patio perfect for contemporary entertaining.

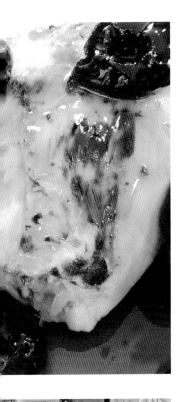

Stuffed Chicken Breasts with Cherry Sauce

Candace says this special occasion dish "is a perfect year-round alternative to stuffed turkey with cranberry sauce." It's also an ideal entrée for when you want to fix something appealing to the eye as well as the palate. The sage-flavored rice stuffing compliments the sweet glaze, and whole cherries add both color and drama. It's a favorite when it's the Milligans' turn to host monthly dinners for the neighborhood gourmet club.

3 tablespoons butter
1/3 cup finely chopped onion
2 tablespoons diced celery
2/3 cup long-grain rice
1/2 tablespoon ground sage
1 1/4 cups chicken broth
4 boneless, skinless chicken breasts
1 cup Sauternes (or any good white dessert wine)
1 small onion, quartered
1/2 cup honey
1/3 cup orange juice
1/2 teaspoon ground ginger
16-ounce can dark sweet cherries
5 tablespoons sugar
3 tablespoons lemon juice
1 tablespoon cornstarch
1 tablespoon cognac

Melt the butter in a medium saucepan, add the 1/3 cup chopped onion and celery and cook until tender. Add the rice and sage; cook and stir until the rice is golden. Slowly pour in the chicken broth and bring the mixture to a boil; reduce heat and simmer for 25 minutes or until all of the liquid is absorbed and the rice is tender. Cut the chicken breasts in half lengthwise and gently flatten each piece with a meat mallet. Top each piece with 1/4 cup of the rice, fold in the sides, roll up and secure with wooden toothpicks. Place in a baking dish with the Sauternes and quartered onion, and bake, uncovered, at 325 degrees for 30 minutes. Stir together the honey, orange juice and ginger and spoon over the chicken; bake for another 10 minutes, or until cooked all the way through. Drain the cherries, reserving 2/3 cup of the syrup; whisk together the reserved syrup, sugar and lemon juice in a small saucepan and bring to a boil. Dissolve the cornstarch in 1 tablespoon cold water and stir into the hot liquid. Once the mixture has thickened, add the cherries and cognac and warm through. Transfer the chicken breasts to a serving plate and top with cherry sauce. Serves 8.

Chocolate Chess Pie

A deliciously simple dessert, this classic pie is ideal for holidays and every day. It's a favorite of the Milligans' son, Colin, who always insists on making it himself.

1 1/2 cups granulated sugar
3 1/2 tablespoons cocoa powder
2 eggs, beaten
2/3 cup evaporated milk
1/4 cup melted butter
1 1/4 teaspoons vanilla extract
1/4 teaspoon salt
9-inch prebaked pie shell

Preheat oven to 325 degrees. In a medium bowl, combine the sugar, cocoa, beaten eggs, evaporated milk, melted butter, vanilla extract and salt; stir until smooth. Pour the mixture into the pie shell and bake for 50 minutes, or until the entire surface puffs up. (If the crust starts to get too brown, you may need to cover the outer edge with foil.) Remove from the oven and cool on a wire rack. Cut into wedges and serve topped with a scoop of vanilla or butter pecan ice cream. Serves 8.

KENDRICK HOUSE

When Thomas and Nancy Woodcock moved to their home on Old Louisville's First Street in 2001, they didn't have far to go at all – because for the nine years prior to that, they had lived next door in the house immediately to the north. Although the move was a short one, the jump in architectural styles was considerable, and today the Woodcocks live in Arts and Crafts splendor in the midst of a neighborhood known for its Victorian ladies.

Built in 1910, their spacious residence has some 5,000 square feet of living space, in addition to an attractive carriage house and an inviting front porch. The first occupant of the home was William Carnes Kendrick, a Louisville jeweler whose father was a renowned American silversmith, and the family name still lives on in the well-known firm of Merkley Kendrick Jewelers. Today, a large built-in display cabinet once showcasing Kendrick silversmithing treasures remains a focal point of the dining room, an elegant yet simple space that has been adorned with golden-hued floor-to-ceiling murals. With the pickled oak woodwork and the stunning bank of original stained glass windows letting in the late afternoon sun, it's easy to understand why Nancy says it's her favorite room in the house.

Pumpkin Bread

Nancy and her family enjoy this tasty pumpkin bread all year long – at breakfast, lunch and dinner. "If I make it at night," she says, "one of the loaves is gone by the time morning rolls around." To make sure you've got enough for your entire family, you might want to double this easy recipe.

3 1/2 cups all-purpose flour
2 teaspoons baking soda
1 1/2 teaspoons salt
1 teaspoon cinnamon
1 teaspoon grated nutmeg
3 cups granulated sugar
4 eggs
2/3 cup water
2 cups canned pumpkin
1 cup vegetable oil
1 cup raisins
1 cup chopped walnuts

Sift the flour, baking soda, salt, cinnamon, and nutmeg together in a large mixing bowl. In a separate bowl, mix together the sugar, eggs, water, pumpkin and oil and add to the flour mixture. Add the raisins and walnuts, and stir to remove all lumps. Divide the batter between two greased loaf pans and bake at 350 degrees for about an hour, or until a pick inserted in the center comes out clean. This recipe makes 2 large loaves that will feed a crowd.

Spicy Rice and Cheese Casserole

The addition of jalapeño pepper and paprika gives this tangy rice dish a pleasantly spicy flavor that is not overpowering in the least. Serve it as a side along fried chicken or roast pork, or enjoy it as a main course with a nice tossed salad and crusty white bread.

1 cup long-grain white rice
Chicken broth
1 cup sour cream
1 1/2 tablespoons jalapeño pepper, seeded and minced
1 1/2 tablespoons jalapeño pepper juice
1/3 cup creamy Italian dressing
1 cup sliced water chestnuts
1/2 pound pepper jack cheese, grated
Paprika

Cook rice according to the package directions, substituting chicken broth for water. Once the rice has cooked, stir in the sour cream, jalapeño pepper, jalapeño pepper juice, Italian dressing and water chestnuts. Spoon half of the mixture into a greased 2-quart casserole and top with half of the cheese. Top with the remaining rice and a second layer of cheese. Sprinkle with paprika and bake, uncovered, at 350 degrees for 30 minutes. Serves 8.

MACAULAY HOUSE

When construction started on the Fourth Street home of Dr. Lawrence and Ricky Gettleman around 1885, Louisville was a growing city in the national spotlight. Already in its third year, the famed Southern Exposition had attracted more than a million tourists, and today's Old Louisville was a neighborhood bustling with activity. Strollers promenaded along Third Street and mule-drawn street cars traveled busy Fourth Street, delivering throngs of visitors to the entrance of the massive exhibit building that stood directly across from this comfortable Queen Anne house.

Since taking up residence in 1990, the Gettlemans have discovered many intriguing tidbits about their house, thanks in no small part to Dr. Evelyn Rich, who wrote a comprehensive history for them in 1997. Former occupants include well-to-do spice merchant, J.D. Macaulay, and his wife Fannie Caldwell Macaulay, the first owners. The aunt of Alice Hegan Rice, the renowned local author of *Mrs. Wiggs of the Cabbage Patch*, Fannie Caldwell achieved her own degree of literary success with six novels and a book on textiles she wrote while living in Japan and Louisville.

The Gettleman's interest in Old Louisville extends beyond the history of their house, however, and they are active members in the community. In addition to the Holiday House Tour and the Hidden Treasures Garden Tour, they look forward to annual neighborhood events such as the Garvin Gate Blues Festival and the St. James Court Art Show.

Bananas Foster

A fan of New Orleans food, Ricky likes to serve this classic dessert when entertaining family and friends. Enjoy it with vanilla or cinnamon ice cream.

2 tablespoons butter
4 tablespoons light brown sugar
2 ripe bananas
1/2 teaspoon ground cinnamon
1 tablespoon banana liqueur

In a large saucepan over medium heat, melt the butter and add the brown sugar; stir and cook for about 5 minutes or until caramelized and deep brown. Add the bananas, which have been cut into large chunks, and cook for 1 minute; stir in the cinnamon and banana liqueur before spooning over scoops of ice cream. Serves 4.

Vegetable Frittata

This Italian omelet is easy to prepare and can be enjoyed any time of day. For a nice supper, serve a wedge of frittata with a tossed green salad and crusty white bread. Ricky's favorite oyster and artichoke soup makes a nice addition.

1 large red pepper, chopped
1 cup sliced fresh mushrooms
1 1/2 cups shredded Swiss cheese
1/4 pound fresh asparagus, chopped
7 large eggs
1/2 cup mayonnaise
1/2 teaspoon kosher salt
2 teaspoons dried basil

Lightly grease a large pie plate and spread the pepper, mushrooms and half the cheese over the bottom; top with asparagus and the remaining cheese. In a large bowl, whisk together the eggs, mayonnaise, salt and basil and pour into the pan. Bake at 350 degrees for 35 minutes, or until a knife inserted in the center comes out clean. Remove from the oven and let rest for 5 minutes before cutting into wedges. Serves 6.

THE ST. JAMES COURT FOUNTAIN

A cherished local icon, the lovely fountain on St. James Court has provided an impressive focal point for the neighborhood since its installation in 1892. Crowned with a graceful female nude perched atop a basin supported by bashful cherubs, it is a partial replica of the Mott Fountain shown at the Philadelphia Centennial Exhibition of 1876. Originally cast in iron, the fountain had largely deteriorated by the 1960s. But thanks to the efforts of Malcolm Bird and others who procured the necessary funds, it was dismantled and recast in bronze at The Fine Arts Sculpture Center in Michigan. A rededication ceremony was held in September 1975, with the addition of a grille work surround that came from the box seats at the old Strand Theater in downtown Louisville.

To see it splashing away during the warm-weather months, most wouldn't realize it, but the fountain is a complicated piece of machinery that requires constant upkeep and maintenance. Thanks to the members of the St. James Court Association, however, its place at the heart of Old Louisville is assured. One of the most recent keepers of the fountain is Dr. Aaron Lucas, a surgeon who lives just a stone's throw away with his wife Rocky in the charming John Starks House.

THE MADISON CAWEIN HOUSE

T"his is a house of books – books read, books written, books loved," says Sena Jeter Naslund, resident of the beautiful Neo-Georgian home on St. James Court. From 2005-2006 the *New York Times* bestselling author served as Kentucky Poet Laureate, an interesting coincidence given that the state's first unofficial poet laureate, Madison Cawein, lived in the house from 1907-1914. Naslund first spied the home in 1973, after moving to Kentucky to teach at the University of Louisville, and many years later – largely due to the success of her novel *Ahab's Wife* – she bought it and moved in. Her library overlooks the splashing fountain on St. James Court, and it has inspired the title of her next novel.

Built in 1901, the year of Queen Victoria's death, the columned, white-washed residence possesses "an architectural beauty that has brought peace and joy" to its inhabitants. During her time here, Sena has penned the novels *The Four Spirits*, *Adam & Eve* and *Abundance, A Novel of Marie Antoinette* – in addition to teaching at nearby Spalding University, where she is program director of the brief-residency Master of Fine Arts in Writing and editor of Fleur-de-Lis Press. Whether enjoying butternut bisque and sea bass in the dining room or crème brûlée with a cup of tea in her sun room, Sena finds the house conducive to spending time with friends and family. She looks forward to many more years in Old Louisville, which she considers "the most architecturally arresting and the most friendly neighborhood" in the city.

Spicy Ginger Butternut Bisque

Sena loves the mildly spicy backdrop achieved with a generous sprinkle of white pepper in this recipe. Combined with the fragrance of ground ginger and the sweetness of honey, the pepper adds a warm note to this creamy squash soup.

7 cups chicken broth
3 butternut squash, peeled, deseeded and diced (about 12 cups)
6 cloves garlic, smashed
1 tablespoon ground ginger
1 tablespoon kosher salt
2 1/2 teaspoons ground white pepper
2 bay leaves
1/2 cup honey
2 cups half-and-half
Crème fraîche for garnish

In a large stock pot, simmer the chicken broth with the squash, garlic, ginger, salt, white pepper and bay leaves for 30 minutes, or until the squash is fork tender. Remove the bay leaves. Add the honey and half-and-half, and use an immersion blender to purée until perfectly smooth. Correct the seasoning and ladle into soup bowls and garnish with crème fraîche before serving. Serves 6.

83

Roast Sea Bass with Cranberry Beurre Blanc

With its mild flavor and flaky texture, sea bass is a popular choice for seafood lovers and fish skeptics alike. Sena and her daughter and son-in-law, Flora and Ron Schildknecht, enjoy this simple preparation, which relies on roasting with butter at a high heat to let the natural flavors of the bass shine through. An elegant beurre blanc rounds out this dish with the tartness of white wine and cranberries. For a nice compliment, serve with a chilled dry rosé.

6 sea bass filets
1/2 cup dry white wine
6 tablespoons butter
Kosher salt
Cracked black pepper

Preheat oven to 400 degrees. Place the fish filets in a shallow baking dish with the white wine. Top each piece with a pat of butter and sprinkle with a pinch of salt and pepper. Roast on a top rack in the oven for 10 minutes; then turn off the oven and place the fish under a broiler for 5 minutes or until the top has browned. Drizzle each filet with a spoon of Cranberry Beurre Blanc and serve with buttered haricots verts and oven-roasted potatoes. Serves 6.

Cranberry Beurre Blanc

A beurre blanc, which translates as "white butter" in French, is a popular wine-based sauce often used to dress up fish and white meat. White wine is reduced with something tart, like vinegar, and then cold butter is whisked in to emulsify the mixture and produce a sauce that is both rich and velvety. This recipe relies on the added tartness of fresh cranberries for a twist on the original.

1/2 cup sauvignon blanc
1/4 cup apple cider vinegar
1/4 cup whole fresh cranberries
1 stick butter, cut into 8 pieces
Kosher salt

In a saucepan over medium heat, cook the sauvignon blanc and vinegar until the liquid has reduced by half; add the cranberries and cook for 5 minutes, or until the berries have broken down and about 3 to 4 tablespoons of sauce remain. Reduce the heat to low, and, one at a time, whisk in each piece of butter until it melts and emulsifies into the cranberry mixture. After all the butter is used, add salt to taste and serve over roasted sea bass. If the beurre blanc is too tart for you, add a teaspoon of honey for sweetness. This beurre blanc will hold for about 30 minutes; if it breaks, stir in a tablespoon of heavy cream and gently reheat.

Lemon Crème Brûlée

Although the fresh citrus in this classic custard dessert makes an ideal end to any seafood meal, Sena and her family enjoy it with most anything – or just by itself with a cup of tea in the afternoon. When serving, Sena likes to use a wide assortment of pottery tableware purchased from artists at the St. James Court Art Show; each October, the fair attracts hundreds of thousands of visitors to the streets of Old Louisville.

2 1/4 cups heavy cream
Zest of 1 lemon
8 large egg yolks,
  at room temperature
1/2 cup granulated sugar
1 teaspoon salt
Juice of 1 lemon
1 teaspoon vanilla extract
Sugar for the top

In a small saucepan over low heat, simmer the cream with the lemon zest for 5 minutes and let cool. In a large bowl, whisk the egg yolks with the sugar until pale yellow and frothy, about 5 minutes. Add the salt, lemon juice and vanilla extract and whisk in the cooled cream until incorporated. Strain the mixture through a sieve and divide among 6 ramekins. Place the filled ramekins in a warm-water bath in a 275-degree oven and cook for 50 minutes, or until the custard has set up. Turn off the oven and let cool in the water bath for another hour before removing from the oven. When completely cooled, top each with a thin layer of sugar and caramelize with a kitchen torch. Serves 6.

THE MOSES AND SOPHIE KOHLER

uilt around 1895, the Third Street home of Mary Martin and Stanley Murrell was originally built as a Victorian "spec house" by the C.C. Mengel Jr. & Bro. Co., the world's largest manufacturer of wooden boxes and containers. In addition to places such as Mexico, the Mengels shipped lumber from family mills in Belize and Honduras, the source for the abundant woodwork in this remarkable Old Louisville mansion. Inlaid hardwood floors in diverse patterns ornament each room, where details such as hand-carved fireplace mantels and coordinating trim of quarter-sawn oak, bird's eye maple, and cherry can be found.

According to the original deeds, C.C. Mengel Jr. & Bro. Co. sold the property to Moses S. Kohler, a milliner, and his wife Sophie in 1896 "for $7,400 cash-in-hand." Situated on a block with some of the most envied dwellings in the neighborhood, the Kohler residence exemplifies many traits of Queen Anne architecture with its steeply pitched roof, three-story turret, seven-bayed windows, and elegant details. One of these details, a salamander perched under a third-floor gable, hints at Châteauesque influences as well.

The symbol of Francis I of France, the king known for building many chateaus, the salamander also symbolizes enduring faith – something the current owners had when they purchased the home in 1990. Hastily erected walls from its days as an apartment house needed to be removed and grand doorways had to be refitted with pocket doors discovered in the cellar. And aside from a gaping hole in the entry hall floor, the front stairwell was in ruins and needed to be rebuilt, Eastlake spindles and all. Today, the grand stairway with its landing and ornate curved stained glass windows is a focal point of the lovingly restored home.

Bobal's Potato Salad

Aunt Bobal was a home economics teacher is small-town Kentucky, who carried her recipes with her when visiting relatives. Her potato salad has been a favorite at family picnics for over 60 years.

5 large red potatoes, cooked
2 teaspoons sugar
2 teaspoons white vinegar
1/4 cup chopped green onion
1/4 cup diced celery
2 tablespoons chopped pimento
4 hard-cooked eggs, sliced
1 cup mayonnaise
1/2 cup sour cream
3 teaspoons kosher salt
1/2 teaspoon ground black pepper

Peel and dice the potatoes and toss with the sugar and vinegar in a large bowl; let marinate for 30 minutes. Add the green onion, celery, pimento, eggs, mayonnaise, sour cream, salt and pepper and lightly combine. Garnish with halves of hard-cooked egg. Serves 6.

Judy's Independence Day Chicken

Mary and Stan began enjoying this dish in the 1960s, when their friend Judy would bring it to lakeside Fourth of July outings. Adapted from a *Bon Appétit* recipe, Judy's summery version remains a year-round favorite and can be served hot or cold.

1 whole chicken
1 pound chopped fresh spinach, cooked
1/2 cup butter, softened
1/3 cup ricotta cheese
1/3 cup grated Swiss cheese
1/3 cup grated Parmesan cheese
1 egg
1/4 teaspoon grated nutmeg
1 teaspoon kosher salt
1 teaspoon black pepper
1/4 teaspoon nutmeg
2 tablespoons olive oil
1/2 teaspoon paprika
1/2 teaspoon oregano
1/2 teaspoon thyme
1/2 teaspoon marjoram

Use a sharp knife to remove the backbone and flatten the chicken. Being careful not to tear the skin, use the point of the knife to loosen the skin from the flesh. In a large bowl, combine the spinach, butter, ricotta, Swiss and Parmesan cheeses, egg, nutmeg, salt and pepper and stuff the spinach mixture into the area between the skin and meat. Place on a rack in a roasting pan and tuck the wings under to avoid burning; mix together the olive oil, paprika, oregano, thyme, and marjoram and rub over the chicken to coat well. Bake at 350 degrees for 1 hour and enjoy. Serves 6.

Summer Ratatouille

A staple at Independence Day picnics, this vegetarian recipe was served with a jug of wine, a loaf of French bread and brownies. For the owners of the Queen Anne home, one taste of ratatouille is a reminiscence of picnics past. For an attractive presentation, lay the roast chicken atop a bed of ratatouille on a colorful serving platter.

1 cup sliced zucchini
1 cup diced eggplant
1/2 cup cherry tomatoes
1/2 cup chopped green pepper
1/4 cup chopped onion
1/4 cup French dressing

In a saucepan over medium heat, combine the zucchini, eggplant, tomatoes, green pepper, onion and dressing. When the mixture starts to boil, turn off the heat and let rest, covered, for 10 minutes. Season with salt and pepper and enjoy at room temperature. Serves 4.

Two marble Chinese lions seem to roar a greeting at the entrance to this stately green-shuttered mansion on South Third Street. Named the "Lion's End," the 7,700-square-foot Federalist-style building was built in 1903 for Oscar Fenley and his wife Mary Woolley Fenley. Mr. Fenley was the President of the National Bank of Louisville and served on the first Board of Directors for the Federal Reserve in St. Louis. The Fenley family resided in the home until 1938 when it became The Carlton Gentleman's Club.

Today the house belongs to John Martin, the Chair of the Harrington College of Design in Chicago, who purchased it in 1998 "as a residence to support the arts." Attracted by the plain symmetry, John finds that the huge light-filled entry hall and over-size living and dining rooms create an ideal setting for his collection of paintings, prints, photography and sculpture. It's an eclectic assortment that includes modern and traditional art as well as Asian and African ceremonial masks, Buddhist offering bowls and Asian furniture.

John's Cocoa-Coffee Brownies

1/2 cup cold butter
1/4 cup oat bran
3/4 cup unbleached
   all-purpose flour
1/4 cup sugar
1/2 cup unsweetened cocoa
1/4 cup all-purpose flour
1/4 teaspoon cinnamon
1/8 teaspoon
   finely ground black pepper
1/2 teaspoon baking powder
14 ounces sweetened
   condensed milk
1 egg, slightly beaten
2 tablespoons Kahlua
1 teaspoon vanilla extract
1 cup chopped pecans

In a large bowl, cut the butter into the oat bran, unbleached flour and sugar and press the mixture into a greased-and-floured 13- x 9-inch pan. Bake at 350 degrees for 10 minutes. In the same bowl, sift together the cocoa, flour, cinnamon, pepper and baking powder. Add the condensed milk, egg, Kahlua, vanilla extract and pecans, stirring to combine. Spread mixture over the cookie crust and bake until the filling sets, approximately 20 minutes. Cool on a rack and cut into squares. Serves 6.

Blueberry Pecan Muffins

1 cup unbleached all-purpose flour
1/4 cup oat bran
1/2 cup sugar
2 teaspoons baking powder
1/4 teaspoon salt
1/2 teaspoon ground coriander
1 egg
1 tablespoon sour cream
1/4 cup milk
1/2 cup chopped pecans
1 cup fresh blueberries
1 teaspoon lemon zest

In a large mixing bowl, stir together the flour, oat bran, sugar, baking powder, salt and coriander. Combine the egg, sour cream and milk and add to the dry ingredients, combining to moisten. Stir in the pecans, blueberries and lemon zest and fill mini muffin cups 2/3 full. Bake at 350 degrees for 20 minutes or until golden brown and enjoy warm. Makes 2 dozen mini muffins.

John's Cherry Chutney

Created by the homeowner, this sweet-and-sour condiment makes the perfect accompaniment to "almost anything," especially white meats such as pork and chicken.

2 1/2 pounds sour cherries, pitted
1 1/2 cups brown sugar
2 medium Vidalia onions, chopped
1 tablespoon mustard seed
1 teaspoon ground ginger
1 teaspoon allspice
1/2 cup white vinegar
1 1/2 cups raisins

In a large saucepan, combine all the ingredients and simmer over medium-low heat until thickened, about 30 minutes. Remove from the heat and enjoy warm or cold.

THE RUSSELL HOUSTON MANSION
Inn at the Park

Architect Maury Mason designed this Richardson Romanesque mansion in 1884 for Russell Houston, one-time president of the Louisville & Nashville Railroad. Herb Warren – he and wife Gayle own the mansion – describes the Richardsonian Romanesque style of architecture succinctly as "turrets, ornaments and fancy brickwork." The residence was saved from the wrecking ball in the early 1970s by preservation devotees including noted Louisville mayor Harvey Sloane. Today, as the Inn at the Park, it is a favorite stop for overnight guests in Old Louisville, and one thing they can always count on is a wonderful breakfast. If you can't make it to this charming bed and breakfast inn yourself, try these recipes at home for a taste of this grand Victorian neighborhood.

For information about the Inn at the Park, contact:

Inn at the Park Bed & Breakfast
1332 South Fourth Street
Louisville, Kentucky 40208
(502) 638.0045
info@oldlouisvilleinns.com

About the Architect

Mason Maury, one of Kentucky's leading architects, was famous for using the Richardsonian Romanesque style, which featured rounded arches over windows and doors, as well as towers and turrets. His artistic legacy includes many fine residential structures in and outside of today's Old Louisville. Maury, who was born in 1847 and died in 1919, was a charter member of the Louisville Chapter of the American Institute of Architects and served as one of its first presidents. Among his early works in the city were the Kauffman Straus Building and the city's first skyscraper, the Kenyon Building.

Innkeeper's Breakfast Popovers

This recipe was inherited from the innkeeper at Louisville's first bed and breakfast, the Old Louisville Inn. The popover, an America cousin of England's Yorkshire pudding, has found an appropriate home in this stunning Victorian mansion. A favorite among guests, the genteel popover makes a regular appearance on the linen and china tablescape at the Inn at the Park.

4 extra large eggs
1 cup whole milk
2 tablespoons unsalted butter
1 cup all-purpose flour
1 teaspoon salt

Preheat oven to 400 degrees. In a medium bowl, whisk together all the ingredients to form a batter; set aside for 15 minutes and stir every 5 minutes to eliminate lumps. Coat 6 popover tins with non-stick spray and divide the batter evenly, filling each at least 3/4 of the way. Bake for 25 minutes. Do not open the door until the 25 minutes have passed. Reduce the temperature to 375 degrees and bake for 20 more minutes. Poke a hole in the top of each popover with a wooden skewer to release the steam and bake for 5 more minutes.

Scrambled Egg Filling

2 tablespoons butter
8 large eggs
1 cup shredded Cheddar cheese
1/4 cup half-and-half
Salt and pepper
Chives, green onion and
   red pepper for garnish

Melt the butter in a heavy skillet over medium heat and whisk together the eggs with the Cheddar cheese and half-and-half. When the butter starts to sizzle, pour in the egg mixture and scramble until the desired consistency is reached. Add salt and pepper to taste. Assemble by using a sharp knife to gently cut a hole in the top of each popover; fill with scrambled eggs and garnish with fresh chives or chopped green onions and slivers of red pepper for color. For a hearty, yet elegant breakfast, serve with strips of bacon and herb roasted potatoes; add a slice of cantaloupe and strawberry for color. Serves 6.

Helga's French Toast with Raspberry Sauce

"I have not had one guest who did not love this French toast served with raspberry sauce," says Helga Vikre, who began experimenting with this recipe 40 years ago – long before she imagined she'd be a resident innkeeper at a Victorian mansion. Like the elegant 1884 bed and breakfast, this recipe has withstood the test of time.

French Toast

5 large eggs, beaten
1/2 cup half-and-half
1/2 teaspoon vanilla extract
1/4 teaspoon grated nutmeg
1/4 teaspoon cinnamon
1 small loaf French bread, sliced
Butter

In a medium bowl, whisk together the eggs with the half-and-half, vanilla extract, nutmeg and cinnamon. Arrange the bread slices in a large baking dish and pour the egg mixture over them; let sit for 5 minutes and use a spatula to carefully turn over each slice so it can absorb more of the egg mixture. Let sit another 5 minutes. Melt some butter on a griddle over medium heat, and fry on both sides until golden brown. Arrange on a serving plate, dust with powdered sugar and drizzle with the Raspberry Sauce. Garnish with whipped cream and a few fresh raspberries. Serve with bacon slices or sausage links. Serves 6.

Raspberry Sauce

10-ounce package frozen red raspberries, thawed
Cranberry juice cocktail
1/3 cup sugar
4 teaspoons cornstarch
Salt
2 tablespoons butter
2 tablespoons orange liqueur
2 teaspoons lemon juice

Drain raspberries and reserve syrup; add enough cranberry juice to syrup to make 1½ cups. Combine the sugar, cornstarch and a pinch of salt and whisk into syrup mixture. Cook over medium heat in a small saucepan, stirring constantly until the syrup is bubbly. Remove from the heat and add the butter, orange liqueur, lemon juice, and berries.

THE SAMUEL CULBERTSON MANSI

The word "palatial" often comes to mind when visitors pass through the front door of this grand dame at the heart of Old Louisville's Millionaires Row. Completed in 1897, the Georgian Revival mansion was home to Samuel Culbertson, one-time president of nearby Churchill Downs. As such, Samuel and his wife Louise entertained a steady retinue of dignitaries from home and abroad, and the lavish third-floor ballroom was reportedly the site of the first official Kentucky Derby party. Though used as a bed and breakfast inn today, the large dwelling has retained its original opulence, much of it drawn from a Renaissance theme of architectural ornamentation with rich woodwork and massive beams visible in areas such as the library, reception hall, and dining room.

And if an illustrious Derby pedigree weren't enough, the residence enjoys a certain literary cachet as well: the mansion provided renowned local author Annie Fellows Johnston with inspiration to write her wildly popular *Little Colonel* books, the second of which, *Two Little Knights of Kentucky,* featured Samuel's sons William and Craig. Over the years, owner Rudy van Meter has amassed an enviable collection of souvenirs and artifacts relating to the famous author and her real-life characters, many of which are proudly on display today.

To reserve your room at the Samuel Culbertson Mansion Bed & Breakfast, contact them at:

Samuel Culbertson Mansion Bed & Breakfast
1432 South Third Street
Louisville, Kentucky 40208
(502) 636-3100
rudy@culbertsonmansion.us

Culbertson Mansion Eggnog

Although this is a popular yuletide beverage, guests at the Samuel Culbertson Mansion enjoy it all winter long. A good dose of bourbon makes this a Kentucky classic any time of year.

12 medium eggs, separated
1 1/4 cups granulated sugar, divided
1 pint good Kentucky bourbon
1/4 cup white rum
1 quart half-and-half
1 quart whipping cream
1/4 teaspoon vanilla extract

In a large bowl, whisk together the egg yolks and 3/4 cup sugar until frothy and pale yellow. Continue whisking and slowly drizzle in the bourbon, followed by the rum and the half-and-half. Whip the cream until stiff and sweeten with 1/4 cup sugar; fold into the egg yolk mixture. Beat the egg whites, 1/4 cup sugar and vanilla extract on high speed until stiff peaks form and fold into the mixture. Refrigerate for several days, making sure to stir carefully once a day, and serve in punch cups topped with a sprinkle of freshly grated nutmeg. Serves 24.

About the Architect

Aside from the Samuel Culbertson Mansion, renowned Minneapolis architect William Channing Whitney (1851-1945) has many other notable projects to his name, including the Minnesota Governor's Mansion and the Minnesota Building at the Columbia Exposition World's Fair of 1893. Appealing to upper-class patrons like the Culbertsons, his tasteful exteriors often housed modern innovations such as electrical refrigeration and intercom systems.

Southern Charlotte

Rudy says this French toast-inspired dish is the most requested breakfast item among his overnight guests. Garnished with sweetened whipped cream and fresh berries, this will become a favorite of yours as well.

12 slices white bread, crusts removed
5 large eggs
2 cups half-and-half
1/2 cup granulated sugar
1 teaspoon vanilla extract

Filling

8 ounces cream cheese, softened
2 large eggs
1/4 cup sugar
16-ounce can peaches, drained
1 teaspoon vanilla extract
2 tablespoons flaked coconut
1/2 teaspoon grated nutmeg

Lay 6 of the slices across the bottom of a buttered 10-by 15-inch pan. In a medium bowl, whisk together 5 eggs, half-and-half, 1/2 cup sugar and 1 teaspoon vanilla extract. Pour half of the mixture over the bread. In a separate bowl, combine the cream cheese, 2 eggs, 1/4 cup sugar, peaches, and 1 teaspoon vanilla extract, and carefully spread over the bread layer. Cover with the 6 remaining slices of bread and pour over the remaining egg mixture. Sprinkle with the coconut and nutmeg, cover and refrigerate overnight.

An hour before serving, preheat the oven to 350 degrees and bake, covered, for 30 minutes; uncover and bake for another 30 minutes, or until puffy and golden brown. Remove from the oven and let stand for 5 minutes before cutting into 12 squares and serving with warm raspberry or maple syrup. Serves 12.

SHARP HOUSE

Ornamental carving beneath the eaves of the gable adds enrichment to the understated façade of this comfortable dwelling from the late 1880s. Its first tenant was J.H. Sharp, the manager of a local carpet company, and its most recent occupants are B. Thomas Thacker and Judith A. Payne, who discovered that the simple interior and exposed brick walls provided an excellent background for their colorful art collection. Contributing to the imaginative décor throughout this Second Street home are the combined furnishings from two previous homes – one in Kentucky and one in British Columbia. Tom and Judy enjoy entertaining and the two recipes that follow are among their favorites.

Flan

Judy received this recipe from María Hardy-Webb, a Cuban friend and Spanish teacher, during a mini-course on Hispanic cooking. It is a favorite of their guests. Although this easy caramel custard serves a crowd, Tom quips there is only one serving: his.

1/4 cup granulated sugar
2 cups whole milk
Zest of 1 lemon
1 stick cinnamon
1/4 teaspoon salt
3 large eggs plus 3 egg yolks
2/3 cup granulated sugar
1 teaspoon vanilla extract

Start with a large ramekin or charlotte pan that can be placed on the stove and in the oven. Melt 1/4 sugar in the pan over medium-low heat, stirring occasionally, until the sugar caramelizes completely and turns light brown. Carefully move from side to side so the caramelized sugar coats the sides. Remove from the heat and set aside to cool. Combine the milk, lemon zest, cinnamon and salt in a saucepan over medium heat and bring to a boil; turn off the heat and cool completely.

In the meantime, whisk together the eggs, egg yolks, 2/3 cup sugar and vanilla extract until frothy; add the cooled milk mixture, stir well and strain through a sieve. Pour the mixture into the caramelized mold and bake in a hot water bath at 350 degrees for 1 hour. Remove from the oven, cool and refrigerate. To unmold the flan, place the casserole in a tray of hot water to melt the caramel on the bottom, top with a large plate and turn over to invert the custard. Garnish with wedges of fresh lime if desired. Serves 8.

Use the 3 extra egg whites to make a large meringue that can be filled with whipped cream and fresh fruit marinated in Cointreau.

Architect's Note: An eave is the edge of a roof; it often projects beyond the side of the building to provide weather protection.

A gable is the triangular portion of a wall between the edges of a sloping roof.

Pumpkin Soup

What began as a way to use up their fall pumpkins over the last 20 years has evolved into a tasty soup that can be thrown together at the last minute. "The guests always scrape their bowls clean," Judy says.

2 cups chicken broth
1 large yellow onion, quartered
4 whole cloves
2 garlic cloves, halved
1 bay leaf, broken in two
2 cups fresh pumpkin purée
Salt and pepper to taste
Juice of 1 lemon
2 cups half-and-half

In a large saucepan over medium-high heat, bring the chicken broth, onion, cloves, garlic and bay leaf to a boil; turn down the heat and simmer, covered, for 10 minutes. Strain out the solids and discard. Use an immersion blender to mix the pumpkin purée, salt, pepper and lemon juice into the broth and simmer for 5 minutes. Add the half-and-half, warm the mixture through, and correct the seasonings. Serves 6.

SLAUGHTER HOUSE

This charming Queen Anne home stands on Sixth Street, at the western entrance of what was once the Southern Exposition. Built around 1889 for William Slaughter, the man who spearheaded the development of St. James Court after the massive exposition building was torn down in the late 1880s, the painted wooden structure was also the residence of John and Christine Gernert, owners of a nearby lumber mill. Other former residents include John and Viola Chickering, and Escue and Geneva Tomerlin, who raised three generations in the house.

In December 2003 sisters Susan Shearer and Linda Gregory purchased the dwelling – it had been divided into four apartments after falling on hard times – and returned it to its former glory. Today, several original stained glass windows provide colorful focal points on the interior, where there are handcrafted details such as hardwood flooring and beautifully carved mantels – one of them with a secret compartment. According to Susan, several spirits became active when the restoration began, and unexplained happenings still take place today. However, instead of being unnerved by the resident ghosts, Susan and Linda have embraced them and the hauntings have been reported in the local media.

German Potato Salad

This straight-forward recipe comes from Susan and Linda's great grandmother, Louise Crandall, a wonderful cook who at one time had a small restaurant in Louisville. One of eleven children born to German immigrants, she was known for her desserts, but this potato salad is a family favorite.

12 medium potatoes
1 cup chopped yellow onion
1/2 teaspoon celery seed
2 teaspoons kosher salt
1/8 teaspoon ground black
  pepper
1 pound bacon, chopped
1/2 cup white vinegar
2 tablespoons sugar
3 tablespoons water
1 egg, beaten
1 tablespoon chopped parsley

Cook potatoes in boiling salted water until tender. Remove from the water and cool slightly; peel and slice into a large bowl. Add onion, celery seed, salt and pepper; lightly toss and cover to keep warm. In a medium-size skillet, cook the bacon until crispy and use a slotted spoon to remove and drain on a paper towel. Stir together the vinegar, sugar and water, and add to the bacon drippings in the skillet. Heat over low heat and when the mixture simmers, slowly pour the mixture into a large bowl with the beaten egg, whisking continuously. Pour over the potatoes and add the bacon and parsley; toss, correct the seasoning and serve warm. Serves 8.

Oatmeal Cake

"Our mother, Betty Russell, got this recipe from a television show in the 1950's; we loved it then and we still love it today," says Susan Shearer. "I can still remember how good the whole house would smell while it was baking." Susan and Linda's sister, Pamela, likes to serve it on Christmas Day, but you'll want to eat it all year long.

1 1/4 cups boiling water
1 cup rolled oats
2 large eggs, beaten
1/2 cup butter, softened
1 cup firmly packed light brown sugar
1 cup granulated sugar
1 1/3 cups all-purpose flour
1/2 teaspoon salt
1 teaspoon baking soda
1/2 teaspoon ground cinnamon
1/2 teaspoon grated nutmeg
1 teaspoon vanilla extract

Topping

1/2 cup butter
1 cup firmly packed light brown sugar
2 egg yolks
1 cup chopped pecans
1 cup flaked coconut
3 tablespoons milk

Pour the boiling water over oats and soak for 1 minute in a large bowl. When cooled, stir in the beaten eggs and mix well. In another bowl, cream the butter with the brown sugar and granulated sugar until light and fluffy; stir in the oat mixture. Sift together the flour, salt, baking soda, cinnamon and nutmeg and add to the oat-butter mixture. Stir in the vanilla extract and bake in a greased loaf pan at 350 degrees for 50 minutes.

To finish the cake, cream together the butter, sugar and egg yolks; stir in the pecans, coconut and milk. Spread over the top of the warm cake and place under the broiler for 5 minutes or until lightly browned. Serves 8.

THE VERNON PRICE MANSION
Central Park Inn

When California residents Eva and Robert Wessels purchased this spacious home overlooking Central Park, they acquired a genuine piece of Old Louisville history. Completed about 1885 for Vernon Price, co-founder of the Price & Lucas Vinegar Manufacturing Company, the 18-room residence sports a distinctive façade covered in rough polychrome fieldstone. Squared columns with carved capitals support the front porch, and the attention to details carries over to the interior where hammered brass hinges, original tile flooring, beautiful art-glass windows and nearly a dozen handcrafted fireplaces await. Today, as the Central Park Inn, this grand dame keeps the grandeur of Old Louisville's Gilded Age alive for the many guests who stay there every year.

To reserve your room at the Central Park Inn Bed & Breakfast, contact them at:

Central Park Inn Bed & Breakfast
1353 South Fourth Street
Louisville, Kentucky 40208
(502) 638-1505
www.centralparkbandb.com

Baked Brie and Mushrooms

Eva says guests always love this impressive appetizer that is actually quite easy to make. You can make it ahead and pop it in the oven at the last minute.

24-ounce round double cream brie
1 1/2 tablespoons salted butter
8 ounces sliced mushrooms
1/2 teaspoon minced garlic
1/8 teaspoon fresh thyme
1/4 teaspoon kosher salt
1/4 teaspoon freshly ground pepper
1 tablespoon all-purpose flour
1 puff pastry sheet
1 large egg whisked together
   with 1 tablespoon water

Preheat the oven to 400 degrees. Remove rind from the brie. Melt the butter in a skillet over medium heat and sauté the mushrooms, garlic and thyme for 15 minutes or until the moisture has evaporated; add salt and pepper and cool. Line a baking sheet with parchment and sprinkle with the flour; lay out the puff pastry and lightly roll out to smooth the surface. Spread the center of the pastry with the mushrooms, making the mushrooms the same size as the brie. Place brie on top and gather together the edges of puff pastry on top to wrap; turn over on to the parchment paper, leaving a smooth finished top with the gathered edges on the bottom. Brush the top and sides with the egg wash and bake for 20 minutes, or until browned. Cool for 10 minutes before serving with a garnish of green and red grapes. Serves 10.

111

Overnight Yeast Waffles with Carmel Maple Syrup

After 10 years of experimenting, Eva thinks she's got the recipe for these airy, perfectly crispy waffles down pat. Her guests tend to agree.

1/2 cup warm water
1/4 ounce active dry yeast
1 tablespoon sugar
2 cups warm whole milk
1/2 cup melted butter
2 cups all-purpose flour
2 large eggs, separated
1 teaspoon vanilla extract
1/4 teaspoon baking soda
1/2 teaspoon kosher salt

Combine the water, yeast and sugar in a glass bowl and let stand 5 minutes; add the warm milk, butter and flour, stirring until completely incorporated. Cover the bowl with plastic wrap and refrigerate overnight, or for 8 hours. When ready to prepare the waffles, whisk together the egg yolks with the vanilla extract, baking soda and salt and mix into the batter. With a hand mixer, whip the egg whites until soft peaks form and fold into the batter. Cook in the waffle maker of your choice until golden and crispy. Drizzle with Caramel Maple Syrup and garnish with whipped cream and fresh berries, if desired. Serves 10.

To prepare the Caramel Maple Syrup, melt 1/2 cup salted butter in a saucepan and add 1 cup whole milk, 2 cups light brown sugar 1/2 cup grade B maple syrup and a pinch of kosher salt. Simmer for 15 minutes, whisking continuously, and serve warm.

Poached Spiced Pears with Lemon Cream

This is another dish Eva has perfected after 10 years of trial and error. According to Robert, it makes a wonderful breakfast starter, or the delicious star of a fruit or dessert course.

2 cups cranberry juice
1 quart water
2 1/2 cups granulated sugar
2 tablespoons ground cinnamon
1 teaspoon grated nutmeg
3/4 teaspoon ground cloves
1 tablespoon vanilla extract
8 fresh whole pears, peeled

In a large pot, bring the cranberry juice, water, sugar, cinnamon, nutmeg, cloves and vanilla extract to a low boil for 15 minutes; reduce the heat and add the pears, simmering for 30 to 45 minutes, or until fork tender. Remove the pears and cool. Serve with Lemon Cream and raspberry syrup, if desired, and garnish with baby mint leaves. Serves 8.

To prepare the Lemon Cream, whisk 1 cup whipping cream until stiff peaks form. In a separate bowl, blend together 4 ounces cream cheese, 1/2 cup sugar, and the juice and zest of 1 fresh lemon until fluffy; fold in the whipped cream.

VICTORIA GARDENS

This 1895 Italianate town home on South First Street is one of four adjacent structures known as Victoria Gardens. These houses were purchased for renovation as part of the historic preservation movement. A major player in this effort was Bob Smith, an interior designer who was responsible for the meticulous restoration of multiple Old Louisville mansions. Today, Victoria Gardens continues as upscale condominiums. This second floor unit blends Victorian character with modern art and amenities. Owners Don Driskell and John Reliford are especially fond of the house's private sculpture garden with lush landscaping, walkways and fountains.

John's Nutty Carrot Cake

3 cups all-purpose flour
2 3/4 cups sugar
1 teaspoon salt
1 teaspoon baking soda
2 1/2 teaspoons ground cinnamon
1/2 cup unsalted butter, melted
2 large eggs
1 cup vegetable oil
1 teaspoon vanilla extract
2 cups chopped walnuts
1 cup shredded coconut
1 1/2 cups mashed carrots
1 cup crushed pineapple, drained
2 packages (8 ounces each)
  cream cheese, softened
2/3 cup butter, softened
6 cups powdered sugar
2 1/2 teaspoons vanilla extract

Sift flour, sugar, salt, baking soda and cinnamon together into a large bowl. Add butter, eggs, oil, and vanilla extract and beat well. Stir in the walnuts, coconut, carrots and pineapple and divide batter among 2 greased 9-inch cake pans. Bake for 35 minutes at 350 degrees or until edges pull slightly away from pan. Cool completely on wire racks. For the icing, beat cream cheese and butter together; add the powdered sugar and the 2 1/2 teaspoons vanilla extract, and beat for 5 minutes. Chill for 30 minutes. To assemble the cake, frost the bottom layer completely and put it in the freezer for 10 minutes until set. Add the second layer and finish by frosting the top and sides. Garnish with extra walnuts, if desired, and chill for an hour before enjoying. Serves 10.

115

THE WILLIAM J. DODD HOUSE

This inviting Arts and Crafts residence sits amicably next to its Victorian neighbors on historic St. James Court. Noted architect William J. Dodd built the three-story stucco house for himself and his wife Ione Estes in 1911. The Arts and Crafts style was a rejection of the beauty-for-beauty's sake ornamentation of Victorian architecture, and this red-tile design features elements typical of the period: built-in cabinetry, art glass windows, and a geometry of mahogany beams. By 21st century standards, its design is simply elegant. Since 2006 owners John and Kimberly Crum have lived here; although the house has many charms, they are especially fond of the Byzantine fireplace mantel in the home's original library.

About the Architect

Canadian-born William J. Dodd was an American architect and designer who worked in Louisville from 1886-1912; from 1913-1930 he was active in Los Angeles, California. Representative of the architectural and design innovations of the late 19th and early 20th centuries, Dodd's works include architecture, functional and decorative architectural glass, furniture, and literary illustration. In a prolific career that spanned five decades, Dodd produced numerous structures, many of which survive today. The best known of these include the original Presbyterian Seminary building (now Jefferson Community & Technical College) and the Weissinger-Gaulbert Apartments, both in downtown Louisville. In Louisville, he designed the Seelbach Hotel and the Western Branch of the Free Public Library as well. He was also one of the architects who drew up the plans for the opulent Fersuson Mansion, today's Filson Historical Society.

117

Priscilla's Hungarian Goulash

Often prepared by Kim's mother Priscilla, Hungarian Goulash remains a favorite family recipe, especially among men. Like the Arts and Crafts home in which the dish is now prepared, this savory stew is both simple and exotic.

3/4 cup butter
1 large onion, chopped
1 garlic clove, minced
3/4 teaspoon lemon zest
1 heaping teaspoon
    caraway seeds
2 heaping teaspoons marjoram
1/4 cup tomato paste
1 cup beef stock
2 tablespoons
    Hungarian sweet paprika
2 pounds stew beef,
    cut in cubes

Melt butter in a heavy pot or Dutch oven over medium heat and sauté the onion and garlic until translucent. Add the lemon zest, caraway seeds and marjoram and stir in the tomato paste to incorporate. Cook for 2 minutes, stirring constantly. Reduce the heat and add stock, paprika and beef; cook, covered, for 2 hours, checking frequently. Uncover for the last 30 minutes to reduce the sauce. As the sauce reduces, one may add red wine. For a thicker goulash, add a tablespoon of cornstarch and stir. Serve over buttered egg noodles and with a green vegetable for color contrast. Garnish with fresh cranberries. Serves 4.

Egg Noodles

3 cups all-purpose flour
1 teaspoon kosher salt
6 egg yolks, beaten
1 teaspoon olive oil
1 tablespoon salted butter

Stir together the flour and salt in a large stainless steel bowl. Make a well in the center of the flour mixture and add the egg yolks and olive oil, using a fork to gradually work in the flour until incorporated. If the dough appears too dry or too wet, you may add additional flour or water as needed. Turn out onto a lightly floured surface and knead the dough until elastic and pliable. Roll out to 1/8-inch thickness and cut the sheet into 2-inch by 2-inch squares, rerolling the scraps until all the dough has been used. Stack the squares one atop the other and use a sharp knife or pastry cutter to cut into 8 strips. Use your fingers to separate the noodles and drop into a pot of salted, boiling water. Cook for about a minute, or until the noodles float to the surface. Drain and transfer the noodles to a large bowl and toss with the butter. Add salt and pepper to taste. Serves 6.

A report by the Louisville Landmarks Commission describes this 7,000-square-foot residence as having ". . . refined Richardson detailing, with particularly exquisite carving in the gable, and foliage enlivening the corners of the massive porch with its squat Romanesque columns." Designed by renowned architect Mason Maury around 1887 for Williamson and Alice Bacon, the mansion and its neighbor to the south have gained a reputation over the years as two of the finest examples of Richardsonian Romanesque Revival houses in the country. Yet despite their claim to fame, both structures were slated for demolition in the 1970s, to make room for a parking lot. When the Kentucky Supreme Court stopped the wrecking ball as a result of the actions taken by local preservationists, the rebirth of Old Louisville gained momentum.

When Susan Coleman and Jeff Layman purchased the deteriorating mansion in 1993, it had been uninhabited for 20 years. Not only were windows boarded up and box gutters rotted away, water damage had forced plaster from ceilings and walls, and floor joists sagged. In addition, squatters had burned holes in the floor and thieves had stripped the house of lighting fixtures, finials, newel posts, stained glass windows and fireplace tiles. But, hope, vision and hard work triumphed in the end and the redbrick residence once again occupies a position of prominence in the neighborhood. In 1995, the Preservation Alliance gave Susan and Jeff an award for the restoration of the mansion, a comfortable family home that blends contemporary sparkle with Victorian appeal.

Asian Salmon with Cilantro-Lime Dressing

1/2 whole salmon, cleaned and de-boned
3 tablespoons granulated sugar
2 teaspoons cracked black pepper
1/2 teaspoon sea salt
1/2 teaspoon wasabi powder
2 tablespoons freshly grated gingerroot
4 tablespoons chopped fresh cilantro
4 stalks lemon grass, thinly sliced
2 fresh red chilies, seeded and
    finely chopped
2 tablespoons rice wine vinegar
2 teaspoons soy sauce
Juice and zest of 2 limes

This dish was a customer favorite at Leander's, a restaurant Susan and Jeff once owned in Old Louisville. It can be served cold over an assortment of salad greens and garnished with wasabi peas and sliced pickled ginger, or it may be served warm atop Asian noodles.

Place salmon filet in a large shallow dish and gently rub with a mixture made by combining the sugar, pepper, salt, wasabi, ginger, cilantro, lemon grass, chilies, vinegar, soy sauce, lime juice and zest. Cover and marinate in the refrigerator for up to 5 days. For a longer marinate, the salmon needn't be cooked; slice thinly on the bias, and drizzle with Cilantro-Lime Dressing. If marinated less than 2 days, or you prefer temperature-cooked fish, grill it for about 2 minutes on each side and serve warm with dressing. Serves 6.

Cilantro-Lime Dressing

Juice and zest of 2 limes
4 tablespoons rice wine vinegar
1 teaspoon soy sauce
1 tablespoon honey
1 teaspoon wasabi powder
1 tablespoon freshly grated gingerroot
3 tablespoons chopped fresh cilantro
4 tablespoons olive oil
Sea salt and coarsely ground black
    pepper

In a large mixing bowl, whisk together the lime juice, zest, vinegar, soy sauce, honey, wasabi, ginger and cilantro; continue whisking and slowly drizzle in the olive oil to emulsify the dressing. Add salt and pepper to taste and serve with the salmon.

121

Caesar Salad

Variations on this classic salad depend on tastes. Jeff and Susan like to use lots of garlic and lemon juice, believing that you can't have too much of either.

2-ounce can anchovies
5 cloves garlic, pressed
2 tablespoons lemon juice
1 tablespoon Worcestershire sauce
1 teaspoon Dijon mustard
3 tablespoons fresh parsley, chopped
1/2 teaspoon freshly ground black
   pepper
1/4 cup olive oil
1 head romaine lettuce
1/4 cup freshly grated Parmesan
   cheese
Croutons

In a large wooden bowl, use a fork to mash the anchovies and garlic into a paste; whisk in the lemon juice, Worcestershire sauce, mustard, parsley and pepper. Continue whisking and drizzle in enough olive oil to make a creamy dressing. Wash the lettuce and tear into pieces and toss in the bowl with the dressing. Top with Parmesan and croutons and enjoy. Serves 6.

123

WOLFE HOUSE

I t's hard to imagine this stately 1890s Richardson Romanesque townhouse as "five awful apartments and a sleeping room," but such was the mansion's fate – that is, until Jim Redmon purchased it in 1979. According to Jane, his wife of 30 years, her mother suggested setting fire to it and starting over; the young couple, however, fortunately ignored this advice and remodeled the first floor in time for their wedding reception in 1980. Subsequent remodeling followed in 1982, 1983 and 1989 – along with three children. In the process the family discovered elaborately painted plaster walls – jungle scenes in the front hall, ribbons and cupids around the ceilings – as well as a child's growth chart from the 1890s. The original cherry wood staircase, ornate fireplace surround, and beautiful stained glass have been preserved as well. Of enduring interest to the owners are the occasional sightings of "three or four small elderly ladies who seem shy, vanishing with any attention given them."

Roast Pork Loin with Sinner's Stuffing

In Kentucky, home cooks often use bourbon to tenderize and flavor everything from appetizers to desserts. Bourbon makes this pork roast "sinfully good." A stuffing of whiskey-marinated dried fruit makes the dish both wholesome and decadent. Pork loin can be presented whole, to be carved by the host, or sliced, plated, and garnished for an elegant buffet.

1 cup pitted prunes, halved
1/2 cup dried apricots, halved
1 cup bourbon
1 teaspoon grated lemon rind
1 teaspoon grated orange rind
1/2 apple, peeled and cut into ½-inch chunks
1 tablespoon honey
4-to 5-pound pork loin roast, boned and butterflied
Salt and pepper to taste
1 garlic clove
4 tablespoons unsalted butter, softened
1 tablespoon dried thyme
2 tablespoons all-purpose flour
1 1/2 cups apple cider

Preheat oven to 325 degrees and soak the prunes and apricots in a bowl with the bourbon for at least 2 hours, until fruits have absorbed most of the liquid. Add lemon and orange rind, chopped apple and honey; mix gently. Reserve extra liquor. Open pork loin and sprinkle with salt and pepper. Lay fruits in a strip down the middle, stopping a few inches from each end of the loin, so as to prevent fruit from falling out when meat is rolled. Gently roll meat up around fruit and tie securely with butcher's twine at 2-inch intervals. Cut garlic into slivers and use a sharp knife to punch deep slits in the surface of the roast; insert garlic in the slits. Rub the roast with butter and sprinkle with thyme; dust rolled pork loin with flour. Place the roast with the cider and reserved bourbon in a large roasting pan in the center of the oven; roast 25 minutes per pound, basting frequently and adding more cider or water if necessary. Remove the pan from the oven, cover loosely with foil and let rest for about 20 minutes before carving. Spoon pan juices over each slice and garnish with fresh grapes and sprigs of thyme. Serves 8.

Beef Wellingtons

Each guest receives a personal Wellington. "This recipe is so much easier than it looks," says Jane Redmon. She and Jim first served this easy dish in 1980 to celebrate the initial renovation of their Victorian mansion.

6 filet mignons, about 1 inch thick
Salt and pepper to taste
6 slices fois gras
2 packages frozen puff pastry shells, thawed
2 eggs beaten with 2 tablespoons heavy cream

Preheat oven to 375 degrees. Season filets with salt and pepper and evenly spread each with a layer of pâté. On a board, roll out 6 pastry shells until large enough to wrap around individual filets; wrap the filets in the puff pastry (pâté side up), sealing the edges underneath with the egg mixture. Brush with egg wash to give a glossy sheen. Roll out 3 more pastry shells and cut out decorative shapes, decorating each wrapped filet with cutouts; brush again with egg wash. Bake on a cookie sheet for about 20 minutes, or until the pastry is golden brown. Filets will be medium to medium rare. Serve with broccoli spears and glazed carrots, and garnish with parsley and cherry tomatoes. Serves 6.

Aviator Cocktails

This drink with its "beautiful cloudy violet color" is based on The Aviation, a drink introduced in 1916 and popular during the Roaring Twenties when pilots were pioneers of the sky. The Redmons have revised the recipe, substituting vodka for gin and reducing the amount of lemon juice.

3 ounces vodka
1 ounce crème de violette
2 dashes lemon juice
2 dashes maraschino cherry juice

For each cocktail, liberally fill a cocktail shaker with ice and add the ingredients. Shake well for 30 seconds and pour into a martini glass or a pony. Garnish with lemon twist and serve immediately. Makes 1 cocktail.

127

Index

ANNUAL EVENTS IN OLD LOUISVILLE

Garvin Gate Blues Fest

The largest free neighborhood street music festival in Louisville, this two-day event takes place every year on the second Friday and Saturday in October. The Garvin Gate Blues Festival attracts a multi-racial, intergenerational audience to the cozy Garvin Place neighborhood, between Fourth and Sixth Streets. Find out more at http://garvingatebluesfestival.com.

Kentucky Shakespeare Festival

Every summer since 1960, the C. Douglas Ramey Amphitheater in the middle of Central Park has delighted thousands of spectators with its repertoire of Shakespeare productions. Shows are open to the public and admission is free. Get more information online at www.kyshakes.org or call (502) 637-4933.

Old Louisville Hidden Treasures Garden Tour

Every year during the second weekend in July, Old Louisville offers a glimpse of its best-kept secrets as garden lovers visit the private green spaces of the nation's grandest Victorian neighborhood. Order tickets online at www.oldlouisvillegardentour.com or call the Old Louisville Information Center at (502) 635-5244 for more information.

Old Louisville Holiday House Tour

Enjoy the spirit of the yuletide at this cherished holiday event in the heart of Kentucky's largest city and see why people are talking about Old Louisville, America's Victorian Gem. Decked out in holiday finery, private homes and local B & Bs open their doors and invite the public inside on the first Saturday and Sunday in December. Order tickets online at http://holidayhousetour.com or call the Old Louisville Information Center at (502) 635-5244 for more information.

The Spirit Ball

Every year on the Saturday before Halloween, from 8:00 p.m. to midnight, spirits soar as party-goers dance the night away at the Conrad-Caldwell House – the Derby City's most opulent Victorian mansion. Gourmet fare, expertly mixed cocktails, live music, a silent auction and a bourbon tasting are enjoyed amidst the backdrop of costumed splendor at the heart of America's grandest Victorian neighborhood. Order tickets online at www.thespiritball.com or call (502) 636-5023.

St. James Court Art Show

Since 1957, throngs of art lovers have flocked to Old Louisville during the first Friday, Saturday and Sunday in October for one of the largest and most popular juried art shows in the nation. Admission is free to this cherished neighborhood event. For more information, go online at www.stjamescourtartshow.com, call (502) 635-1842 or email mesrock@stjamescourtartshow.com.

CENTRAL PARK

An oasis of green for more than a hundred years, Central Park is located adjacent to picturesque St. James Court in the heart of Old Louisville. Although created by the firm of Frederick Law Olmstead, the designer of Central Park in New York City, Kentucky's version has little else in common with New York's more famous park, other than its shady walkways and inviting natural landscaping. One major difference is that the park was not centrally located when laid out a mile south of the city limits in 1904, and the name most likely originated from the Central Passenger Railway. Originally a mule-drawn line that transported people from the center of town to DuPont Square, the site of the DuPont family estate, the railway made a hefty profit for the DuPonts and proved integral in the development of today's Old Louisville neighborhood.